Amazing Sailing Stories

For Emily

Amazing Sailing Stories

Dick Durham

This edition first published 2011

Registered Office
John Wiley & Sons Ltd, The Atrium, Southern Gate, Chichester, West Sussex, PO19 8SQ, United Kingdom

Editorial Office
John Wiley & Sons Ltd, The Atrium, Southern Gate, Chichester, West Sussex, PO19 8SQ, United Kingdom

For details of our global editorial offices, for customer services and for information about how to apply for permission to reuse the copyright material in this book please see our website at www.wiley.com.

Reprinted December 2011, February 2012

Library of Congress Cataloging-in-Publication Data

Durham, Dick, 1951–
Amazing sailing stories / Dick Durham.
p. cm.
Summary: "A wonderful hardback collection of thrilling stories of the sea, both ancient and modern" – Provided by publisher.
ISBN 978-0-470-97803-0 (hardback)
1. Sailing–Anecdotes. I. Title.
GV811.D84 2011
387.2′04309–dc23

2011029123

ISBN: 978-0-470-97803-0 (hbk) ISBN: 978-1-119-95261-9 (ebk)
ISBN: 978-1-119-95263-3 (ebk) ISBN: 978-1-119-95262-6 (ebk)

A catalogue record for this book is available from the British Library.

WILEY NAUTICAL

Set in 12/14pt Garamond by Aptara Inc., New Delhi, India
Printed in Great Britain by TJ International Ltd, Padstow, Cornwall

CONTENTS

CONTENTS

PART ONE

Survival

VOYAGE OF DESPERATION

With no sailing or navigation experience John Caldwell set out from Panama on a 9 500-mile voyage to get back to his wife in Australia. His voyage included shark attack, starvation and shipwreck

The lack of shipping, at the end of World War II, prompted lovesick John Caldwell to embark on one of the most foolhardy voyages in the annals of sailing history because he was pining for his newly-wed wife Mary. They had married in 1945, but she was back in Sydney, Australia and the boatless Caldwell had come ashore at Balboa, Panama in May 1946 after working as a merchant seaman aboard a US Liberty ship distributing Australian troops to Borneo.

So the 27-year-old Texan bought *Pagan*, a 29 ft cutter which had 1 000 pounds of cement poured into her bilge to help the 600-pound lead shoe nailed onto the keel keep her 40 ft mast upright. She would not have been everyone's choice of craft in which to cross the Pacific Ocean.

With no experience of sailing or navigation other than that which he had managed to glean from a basic book: *How To Sail*, Caldwell set off with two cats, Flotsam and Jetsam for company and 248 tins of food and 95 gallons of water. With the engine running and the helm lashed he walked forward to stow the anchor and cable, but while carrying the anchor he tripped and plunged overboard and went down with the hook until he let go and fought his way to the surface. Here he found his little ship driving round and round the dragging anchor. *Pagan* hit a buoy, as Caldwell swam towards her, but as she took a run at him he managed to scramble up her low freeboard by way of the chain plates. Now with the engine still running and the anchor still dragging he decided to have a go at sailing! After an uncontrolled gybe, he managed to retrieve his anchor and chain, then dropped the sails and motored out to sea. With just 9 500 miles to go before Australia, the solo sailor decided he better get in some practice, but out of sight of the longshoremen of Balboa. Instead Caldwell managed to con the boat to the Perlas Islands on the south-eastern side of the Gulf of Panama and here spent eight days practising. During a gale he managed to hit an uprooted floating tree which sprung some planks. *Pagan* was beached before she sank and Caldwell repaired her and set sail once more for the Galapagos Islands.

About halfway to the Galapagos he decided to have a go at shark fishing: hoping to show off a shark's jaw to Mary. Amazingly and with the use of a halyard he fished and landed a large shark weighing several hundred pounds. He tried killing it with an axe, but this brought the beast back to life and with a flick of its tail snapped off *Pagan's* tiller and flipped it over the side. By the time Caldwell had despatched it the shark had half-demolished the cockpit and wrecked the engine.

In the Galapagos he stopped to clean *Pagan's* hull of weed and barnacles and set off from Floreana for his next destination, the Marquesas 3 000 miles away.

Although he saw Nuku Hiva, the main island and port of clearance for the Marquesas, Caldwell was anxious to push on and try to beat the hurricane season, and so, even after 29 days he did not stop. Instead he called in, briefly, at the Caroline Islands for coconuts to eke out his dwindling supplies. Here he gave away his two cats to some admiring children.

Six days out of the Carolines the weather started to deteriorate. Caldwell feared the worst as squalls started building, the sky got darker and rain drenched the little boat. A full-blown hurricane was about to take over his life. Caldwell stowed his anchor below, put his inflatable dinghy on a painter astern, and lashed everything down including himself to his bunk. There he lay worrying whether *Pagan's* 26-year-old timbers would hold together.

For three days he lay like this as the storm raged about him, ripping out the mast, filling the boat with water and making a quagmire of the tools, food and clothing below.

After it was over Caldwell used the broken spars to make a jury rig and under much reduced canvas carried on, at approximately one knot, hoping to limp into Samoa.

Food ran low and then out. He fried a fish in Vaseline, ate toothpaste, face cream, a stub of lipstick he'd been saving for Mary and 'fried' some chamois leather in shaving cream and engine oil. Then he cut an oar into a spear and managed to catch some fish. But *Pagan's* progress was pitifully slow and he next cut up his leather army boots, 'tenderised' them by beating them on the end of his bunk, soaked them in salt water, then fried them in hair oil before boiling them in strips. He even scraped the seaweed off *Pagan's* stricken hull, 'dressed' it with hair oil and swallowed that, too.

At last a breeze came and he was able to shape a course. After 36 days under jury rig, weak from starvation and lack of water and with no compass or other navigation equipment – they'd been lost or smashed in the hurricane – he ran *Pagan* up on a coral reef off the island of Tuvutha in the Lau Group of the Fiji Islands.

Caldwell eventually managed to stagger ashore across the reef to a beach where he lay exhausted with bits of wreckage from *Pagan* for company.

After three days he was rescued by locals who could only get to him by sea as the cliffs to the hinterland were inaccessible.

He was taken off by a schooner which visited the islands every four months to load copra: she had visited the island just a couple of weeks before so Caldwell went native while waiting. His hosts nursed him back to health.

Eventually, via New Caledonia he flew to Brisbane and finally arrived in Sydney where he was reunited with his wife for the first time in 19 months.

THREE MONTHS ADRIFT IN A RUBBER DINGHY

A middle-class couple's blue-water dream of sailing round the world turned into a nightmare when their boat was sunk by a whale and they spent 118 days clinging to life and hoping for rescue

They were an ordinary couple: he a printer's clerk, she a tax officer, and both lived miles from the sea. But Maurice and Maralyn Bailey had a dream: to sail across the Pacific Ocean in their own boat. The only way they could afford to do this was to sell their house in Derby. With the proceeds they bought a Maurice Griffiths-designed bilge keeler, a 31 ft Golden Hind. She was built in Plymouth and characteristically christened with the union of their own names, *Auralyn*. They taught themselves how to sail and navigate from books and in June 1972 they sailed from the River Hamble, in

Hampshire via the Canaries, to Barbados, Antigua and the Panama Canal before entering the Pacific.

In the early hours of their sixth day out from Panama and steering for the Galapagos Islands they spotted the lights of a whaling ship and steered clear of her after she trained a searchlight on *Auralyn* to warn them away.

Just as the sun was rising their plywood boat was hit by a sperm whale – which naturalist Sir Peter Scott later speculated might have seen *Auralyn* as a source of food – so heavily that Maralyn watched in horror as the creature thrashed around astern of them in a sea of blood.

Water soon started rising through the boat's cabin and to Maurice's horror he discovered a splintered hole 18 ins × 12 ins on the port side. They tried draping a spare sail around the gash and stuffing it with blankets on the inside. But 40 minutes later the boat was settling and they inflated their life-raft tossing jerry cans of water, stores, charts, navigation equipment and food into the inflatable dinghy. From their rubber convoy they took pictures of their new home sinking beneath the waves as a perfect morning established itself.

They lived on the life-raft and used the inflatable dinghy for stores. Maurice rowed the dinghy, towing the life-raft, due south, hoping to make good a course of south-west which would put them among the Galapagos archipelago, but the current and prevailing winds were both from the south-east and they were set 150 miles north of the islands after 22 days.

In this time they spotted a ship, but a malfunctioning flare meant its crew failed to see them. They killed a turtle, and butchered it for food. And they made fish-hooks out of safety pins, using a pair of scissors to fillet the fish they caught. Both forced themselves to eat raw fish and they collected rain water in a bucket from the life-raft's canopy.

Three more ships appeared but steamed on. The last one coming within half a mile but still not seeing the 'bonfire' Maurice had lit in a biscuit tin or the waving of orange oilskins by Maralyn. A fifth ship also failed to spot their, by now, home-made flares of rag and paraffin. And then a small disaster struck when Maurice, while trying to catch a milk fish, punctured the life-raft with his hook. They patched it up but found to their dismay that the life-raft required pumping with air twice a day. Then they discovered that a spinefoot fish, hovering in the shade beneath the raft had also punctured it. They tried unsuccessfully to repair the holes and now noticed the tape joining the two circular tubes of the life-raft had perished in the relentless sun. After the seventh ship passed without seeing them they spent the next six weeks entirely alone on the ocean.

Then, on their 93rd day adrift during a storm, a large wave capsized the inflatable while Maurice was in it baiting hooks for turtle-fishing. He surfaced alongside the upside down dinghy. Maurice managed to scramble into the life-raft and they righted the dinghy but they had lost all their bait and fishing gear. After bouts of diarrhoea they decided on a change of diet and caught and strangled booby birds. But the fish was much too tasty to ignore and after fashioning more fish hooks from safety pins they caught dorados, wolf herring and small sharks. A second storm lasted four days and capsized the inflatable again leaving them just one fish hook and Maurice tried using his navigational dividers opened out as a spear.

On 30 June after 118 days adrift and 43 days after seeing their last ship they were spotted by a Korean tuna fishing boat, *Weolmi 306.* They were given fresh clothes, food and medical attention and dropped in Honolulu, Hawaii, thirteen days later.

The 118 days they spent adrift is still a record in the annals of survival.

THE TRUE STORY OF MOBY DICK

The classic tale of adventure and obsession on the high seas is based on an horrific real-life whaling voyage

One reason Herman Melville's classic story *Moby Dick* is such a wonderful book is that it's fiction based on an even stranger true story. Before writing it the author interviewed a whaling man, Owen Chase, first mate of the Nantucket whaleship *Essex* and was haunted by his grim yarn.

On 20 November 1820 the *Essex* and her 20 crew were 1 000 miles from the nearest land close to the Equator in the Pacific Ocean when they sighted a spout. It marked a pod of whales. The ship was hove-to: one set of sails set in the opposite direction to the others so the ship would stay almost in the same position. This enabled all the sailors to leave the ship and give chase to the whales in their three whaling boats which were lightly built for speed. Captain George Pollock was in charge of one boat, Owen Chase another and the second mate, Englishman Thomas Chappel, the third boat.

Chase was first to impale a sperm whale with his harpoon but the wounded giant thrashed the water with its tail and smashed the planking of his boat. Chase cut the harpoon line with his hatchet and he and his crew baled the leaking boat as they rowed her back to the *Essex*. They hauled the splintered boat on deck and while some started to make repairs others reset the sails of the mother ship and headed towards the other two whale boats.

Suddenly an 85 ft sperm whale broke water 110 yards off the *Essex's* bow and swam towards the ship at an estimated three knots – the same speed as the square rigger.

'The ship brought up suddenly and violently as if she had struck a rock,' Chase wrote and added that having rubbed his back on the keel of the ship the whale came up on the leeward side and lay on the surface 'apparently stunned with the violence of the blow.' But the whale quickly recovered and 'He was enveloped in the foam of the sea, that his continual and violent thrashing about in the water had created around him, and I could distinctly see him smite his jaws together as if distracted with rage and fury.'

The *Essex* began to list, the crew manned the pumps and used flags to signal the other boats but the whale was coming back for a second attack.

'I saw him about 100 yards directly ahead of us, coming down apparently with twice his ordinary speed; and to me, at that moment, it appeared in tenfold fury and vengeance in his aspect,' Chase added. The combined speed of the whale and ship resulted in a nine knot impact.

As Chase and his men pumped and gathered stores together, Captain Pollock and second mate Chappel were horrified to notice the ship had disappeared: she had listed over so far that her masts were below the horizon. They rowed furiously for miles on a compass course back towards the *Essex* before they sighted her.

Once back aboard Pollock ordered the rigging of the masts to be cut so they could be toppled over the side and help the ship right herself. It gave them a little more time to make sails from spare canvas for the three whaling boats and load them with 65 gallons of water each, plus bread, biscuit and turtles. Two compasses and three quadrants were loaded for navigation and for two nights they hung by the slowly sinking *Essex* moored to her stern.

On 22 November they abandoned the *Essex* and set sail for the coast of South America.

After battling high seas for 28 days the three boats spotted land on 20 December: an uninhabited island on which they managed to live off fish, and slaughtered birds. However, apart from a fickle stream which appeared in shoreline rocks at low tide there was no fresh water.

Pollock and Chase decided to move on and try and make for Easter Island. Chappel opted for staying on the island and was joined by two other men.

Pollock and Chase loaded a flat stone as a cooking hearth in one boat and set off on 27 December now with three boats between 17 men.

The three castaways drank the blood of birds and discovered a cave containing eight skeletons: possibly from another shipwrecked crew.

But they survived until 5 April when a gunshot announced the arrival of the ship *Surrey*, which took them to Valparaiso where they learned what had happened to their shipmates.

By 8 February having survived storms, shark attack and being split up in heavy weather, three of the crew had died from their ordeal. The third man was Isaac Cole and the now starving men on Chase's boat cut up his corpse and ate parts of it in desperation.

On 18 February Chase and his crew were picked up by the brig *India* commanded by Captain William Crozier of London. They, too, were taken to Valparaiso.

Captain Pollock and one surviving crewman, veteran whaler George Ramsdale, were also picked up, half-starved, by the American whaler *Dauphin*.

One boat and her crew completely disappeared.

Only eight of the original 20 survived and it was many years before Captain Pollock could bring himself to write his own account. Hardly surprising as he revealed that four men who died were eaten by the others at which point Captain Pollock loaded his pistol and laid it on a thwart of the boat. As their hunger returned the surviving men drew lots as to who would be sacrificed for the next meal. It was the cabin boy Owen Coffin who drew the short straw. Pollock said: 'My lad if you don't like your lot, I'll shoot the first man that touches you.' But the boy replied: 'I like it as well as any other,' and laid his head on the seat. Captain Pollock then gave his last order of the ill-fated cruise. Ramsdale obeyed and shot the lad through the head.

PSYCHOPATHS IN THE FO'C'SLE

Despised as useless steamboatmen and having suffered bullying and abuse from the rest of the crew, two Filipino sailors started a murder spree which ended in the loss of their ship

The forward cabin of a sailing ship, the fo'c'sle, was where the ordinary seamen slept. It was a rough and ready billet where sailors learned to live with one another rubbing along together and making the best of shared accommodation. It was no place for over-sensitive souls, law and order was imposed by cuffs and curses, but it was a great leveller and crews soon found their own place in an unspoken hierarchy. Any weakness in the daily duties of sailing the ship was revealed immediately and not tolerated.

The fo'c'sle of the New York-bound full rigged ship *Frank N Thayer*, when she sailed from Manila in the first week of November 1885 with a cargo of hemp, was a melting pot of different nationalities which included two Filipino seamen. They were steamboatmen who knew nothing about sailing, but who were taken on by Captain Robert Clarke, obliged to make up a crew of 22 hands for the voyage.

Their ignorance of sail was exposed as soon as the ship left port: they did not know the names of the vessel's sails or of the running and standing rigging which made giving commands tedious. Their slight build added little extra weight on the end of a rope, and one European sailor dubbed the pair 'one bloomin' rat power'. They could not steer by the wind and so with one in the port watch and the other in starboard watch they were used by the officers of both for menial tasks only.

They became 'fo'c'sle peggys' the general dogsbodies of the rest of the hands, obliged to fetch and carry for their shipmates.

A well built German sailor forced one of the 'coolies', as unskilled Oriental labourers were then derogatorily called, to swap berths as his suffered from a deck leak. While transferring his gear the Filipino sailor cursed him under his breath in his native tongue. When the German demanded to know what he had said and was told he had been described as a 'square-head' he beat him up.

A few days later his fellow Filipino let the ship run off course and was told by the second mate, Davis, never to come aft to the wheel again. 'All you're fit for is scouring out the hencoop and pigsty,' Davis had said. At which the Asian pulled out a knife. Davis then said: 'If I ever see your knife come out again I'll rub your black face in the deck. Savvy?'

No-one except the Chinese cook, Ah Say, took any notice of the long scar running down the face of one of the Filipinos, and much later it was revealed the other had a criminal record.

Despite the shortcomings of her two steamboat crew, the *Frank N Thayer* made a good run across the Indian Ocean, rounded the Cape of Good Hope and stood northwards into the South Atlantic. She soon picked up the south-east trade winds and with her yards trimmed square, steered for the island of St Helena where Captain Clarke, who had his wife and child aboard, intended to secure fresh provisions.

On the night of 2 January 1886 the *Frank N Thayer* was approximately 700 miles south-east of St Helena making 10 knots under full sail. The starboard watch were having an easy time of it laying on deck on blankets enjoying the full moon and balmy air. The second mate was then approached by the two Filipinos, one of whom asked for medication as he had a 'sick stomach'.

Davis replied that the medicine chest was in the captain's cabin and that he was not going to rouse him over a stomach ache. Both the Filipinos then pulled out their knives and fell upon him. But Davis managed to stagger along the deck and down the companionway to the captain's cabin where, after hammering on the door, he collapsed.

Captain Clarke, horrified to find his second mate's body outside his cabin door rushed on deck still dressed in his pyjamas. As he emerged from the hooded companionway he was gripped by the throat and stabbed in the shoulder. Clarke, who had a reputation for being a 'tough egg' fought back with bare hands but received knife wounds to his head, face and body. Getting weaker from loss of blood, the bold captain gripped his assailant in a body hug and as he started swaying, held the man as both plunged back down the companionway where the captain passed out.

Believing the captain had become victim number two, the Filipinos went back on the now almost empty deck. The first mate Holmes had also been stabbed and had been dragged into the fo'c'sle by the rest of the crew who had then barricaded themselves in.

The captain's wife, using for the first time the Shipmaster's *Medical Guide*, had the book open on the cabin table while she dressed his wounds including a deep gash just below his ribs from which protruded the lower lobe of his lung. Applying a thick antiseptic wad she then bound him up tight with a body bandage which a doctor later reported could not have been bettered by himself.

The pair then heard somebody scuffling about in the main saloon. Captain Clarke armed himself with a ship's revolver and opened the cabin door to find a Norwegian seaman, Hendrickson, pleading for sanctuary.

When the captain discovered only two men were involved with the mutiny he was greatly relieved, but just in case Hendrickson was involved he refused him a berth in his own private quarters, but allowed him instead to hide in the officers' bathroom.

Shortly afterwards Captain Clarke's wife noticed their cabin skylight was slowly being raised letting in a shaft of moonlight. Against the glow they watched a bare foot appear and Captain Clarke raised his gun and fired. The intruder dropped the skylight with a shower of curses. Clarke and his wife next heard the screams of the helmsman as he was knifed, dragged to the rail and thrown overboard.

The two killers now had the run of the ship. The trouble was they could not sail and all those who could were battened down below in fear of their lives. So they carried on with their slaughter, dragging the carpenter from his cabin, knifing him and throwing his body over the side. Next they found the cook hiding in the coal bunker in his galley. But they spared him as they were hungry and as he was Chinese. Ah Say cooked them a meal and was pressed to fall in with the pair. The killers then revealed their plan. They intended to murder the whole crew, throw their bodies overboard, then drop one holed lifeboat into the sea. Upon somehow making port they would claim that they had hidden from mutineers who had eventually left the ship. The two were under the false impression they could then claim salvage.

At about five o'clock on Sunday morning, 3 January, when the killers had been 'in charge' of the *Frank N Thayer* for 29 hours, more screams were heard as they discovered a fourth man who was hiding in the sail locker. He was dragged on deck, stabbed and thrown overboard. After the first mate Holmes died of his wounds in the fo'c'sle, the rest of the crew at last decided to rush the mutineers. Armed with belaying pins, sailor's fids, and other makeshift weapons they rushed out on deck in a body. But, although outnumbered six or seven to one, the street-life past of the killers came into play. After the clash, four men were left wounded, a fifth lay dead with his throat slit and the crew ran back to the fo'c'sle and locked themselves in. But one sailor, Willis, had not been quick enough to reach the sanctuary of the fo'c'sle and so he scrambled aloft. Although the Filipinos had been poor sailors they now showed new-found agility on the ratlines and raced up behind their terrified quarry who climbed higher and higher. At the fore topgallant yard he found a tail block which had been used for bending on a sail but which had not been taken back down on deck. Using this as a mace he swung the heavy block at the heads of the murderers until they gave up the chase and returned to the deck.

The day dragged on with the ship rolling athwart the wind and sea, half her sails in tatters and the rest thrashing noisily. The Filipinos now barricaded the crew into the fo'c'sle from the outside in case they decided on another sortie. They then returned aft with knives lashed to the end of boathooks in a bid to stab the captain through the skylight and obtain his revolvers. Captain Clarke fought them off with shots through the skylight and instead he too was now barricaded into his cabin.

By the following day Captain Clarke was eating and recovering his strength. He now allowed Hendrickson into his cabin and after a thorough cross-examination armed him with a revolver. Using a fire axe Hendrickson smashed down the barricaded cabin door, the noise of which brought the two Filipinos back to the poop deck just as Captain Clarke and Hendrickson emerged. The sight of the gleaming revolvers stopped them in their tracks. The Captain shot one of them square in the chest. He fell, but picked himself up and went to the rail where he clawed at his shirt. Both guns now fired and he pitched headfirst over the rail. The other Filipino had disappeared.

With a shout of triumph Willis came down from his high perch and Ah Say, armed with a meat chopper joined in the hunt for the second killer.

The crew were released from the fo'c'sle and Captain Clarke ordered them to bend on new sails, get the yards trimmed and the ship back on course for St Helena, while he and his posse searched the ship for the missing Filipino.

Nobody had considered the main hold as a hiding place until wisps of smoke were seen curling out of the cowl ventilators. 'The sneaking rat has set fire to the ship,' one of the sailors yelled. A bucket chain gang was formed and water poured into the smouldering hemp.

Soon the remaining killer was smoked out of the hold and he emerged on deck coughing and gasping for breath. Hendrickson who had been guarding the hold fired two shots and the rest of the crew then piled in raining blows on the man. But he managed to wriggle clear, rushed to the bulwarks and leapt over the side and swam away. Hendrickson reloaded and fired at the swimming man's head, the rest of the crew hurled nuggets of coal at him. The ship soon left him behind. But the *Frank N Thayer* was doomed herself. Soon flames were leaping from the hold and Captain Clarke knew his fire-fighting was in vain. So he ordered the sails to be backed while the ships' lifeboat was provisioned. The boat with its 17 survivors pulled away from the blistering side of the ship but remained in the vicinity, hoping the smoke of the blazing ship would be spotted by rescuers. But shortly before sunset, after her masts and spars toppled, the ship stuck her stern skywards and slid beneath the waves with a great hissing sound.

Captain Clark took star sights over the next seven days and nights and safely reached St Helena, although by this time he and the wounded among the crew were in fever and suffering bouts of delirium. All made a full recovery in hospital before the American consul shipped them home.

ONCE IS MORE THAN ENOUGH

Having been pitch-poled in the Southern Ocean and almost sunk, Miles and Beryl Smeeton tried again to round Cape Horn. This time they were capsized

Miles Smeeton, a former British soldier and his wife Beryl had settled in Vancouver on a farm but wanted to sail round Cape Horn 'because it was there'. In 1950, the couple, along with their daughter, Clio, travelled back to their native England by steamer to search for a boat and found the 46 ft Bermudian ketch *Tsu Hang* in Dover. After a refit they crossed the Atlantic to Barbados, then via Panama to Vancouver arriving in June 1952. In 1955 the Smeetons, including Clio, sailed to San Francisco where they met 27-year-old solo sailor John Guzzwell in his home-built 20 ft 6 ins boat *Trekka.* Both boats then set off for the Bay of Islands in New Zealand via Hawaii and the Pacific. *Trekka* was slipped in Russell in the Bay of Islands and

Guzzwell then joined the Smeetons both aged 50 aboard *Tsu Hang* and sailed to Melbourne for the 1955 Olympics. From there Clio flew back to the UK, leaving her parents and Guzzwell to make the ill-fated trip towards the Horn, en route to the UK.

Seven weeks out of Melbourne and 1 000 miles from Cape Horn, they were running through a storm under bare poles and towing a three inch thick hawser as a drogue. Miles had already dismissed the idea of spreading drummed oil astern to try and dampen down the seas when a wall of water with a completely vertical face, down which ran white ripples like a waterfall, came roaring up astern.

It was a wave with *Tzu Hang's* name written on it and down below, Miles was reading in his bunk when the boat was rolled forward and pitch-poled by the wave, which swept away both masts at the deck, and the dinghy and sky-lights. The rudder had also gone, but worst of all, the whole doghouse had been carried away, leaving a big hole in the deck. Less than two feet of her hull was showing above the waves. It seemed like the end and *Tzu Hang* awaited the final blow. The wave had swept Beryl over the side, shearing the steel snap hook on her safety harness, designed to withstand a one-ton breaking strain. She was now 30 yards from the boat with a crushed vertebra, and a deep gash in her forehead. She swam for her life towards the stricken hull and was grabbed by Miles as another wave broke over the hull. He had to shout at John to lend a hand, because the younger man had given up hope any of them would survive. 'I thought it was pointless as we were all going to be gone soon,' John later recalled.

Once Beryl was back aboard, all three took stock of the situation and John, who had built his own 21 ft boat, *Trekka*, in which he was later to sail solo around the world, started to use his shipwright skills to cover the holes in *Tsu Hang's* deck with galvanised nails, a genoa sail, floorboards and cupboard doors. Then all hands bailed for 12 hours and the boat gradually began to rise. Over the next two days John made a 15 ft jury mast scarfed together from two broken headsail booms and a 16 ft steering oar from doorposts and bits of bulkhead, with a locker door as a blade.

In such a crippled state it took *Tsu Hang* 37 days to sail 1 490 miles to Coronel, Chile, arriving on 22 March 1956. She was hauled out in the naval base at Talcahuano, where John rebuilt her from the deck up, after which he returned to the Bay of Islands in New Zealand and *Trekka* to continue his circumnavigation.

On 9 December, nine months after reaching Chile, *Tsu Hang* set off once more for Cape Horn, on passage to the UK, this time two-handed. Dawn on Christmas Day saw Miles and Beryl 500 miles north-west of the Strait of Magellan with a steadily falling glass. The following day as conditions worsened, they stowed all canvas, lashed the tiller to leeward and went below leaving *Tsu Hang* laying ahull.

A large breaking wave gripped *Tsu Hang's* hull and she broached and rolled over. She was dismasted again, but although her dinghy had been swept away, the skylights were not torn off and although the doghouse was stove in on one side this time it was not ripped off. Below the heavy cabin stove had broken loose and both Miles and Beryl sustained head injuries from flying objects.

For two days they repaired the doghouse using floorboards, made a mainmast from the mizzen boom and used the remaining nine feet of mizzen as a sail. Over the next 12 days they made daily runs of 70 or 80 miles with only a vague idea of their position because the radio, barometer and chronometer were smashed beyond repair and their two coastal charts were nowhere to be found: they only had the pages of an American chart catalogue to sail by and without an accurate measure of time they were useless anyway. On 27 January 1957, after 30 days and over 1 500 miles under jury rig, they picked up the lights of San Antonio and sailed into Valparaiso Bay, Chile.

The Smeetons still did not give up their ambition to sail around Cape Horn, and eventually managed to do so before selling *Tsu Hang* in 1968. Many years later and fascinated by the Smeeton's story, their godson, Miles Clark, went to try and find the much battered yacht. He eventually tracked her down to Puerto Rico where she had been hulked after being sunk during a hurricane. The locals call the place: *el cementario del barcos* – the graveyard of ships. In 1990 *Tzu Hang* was broken up and her remains dumped at the city landfill overlooking San Juan. A sad end after 240 000 sea miles, but sound testimony to her design by H. S. 'Uncle' Rouse and construction in 1938 of Burmese teak.

THE GREATEST SEA VOYAGE OF ALL TIME?

Ernest Shackleton's attempt to reach the South Pole on foot was scuppered when his ship was crushed and sunk in pack ice. But he became more famous for the rescue he organised than the record he set out to achieve

Bankers rattle by on the overhead railway, which weaves around the skyscrapers of London's Canary Wharf, never giving a second glance to the sudden opening of water between the glittering towers of money making. But from this spot the seeds were sown of one of the greatest sailing survival stories of all time. In 1914 that patch of water was called West India Dock and it was here the polar exploration ship, *Endurance*, was fitted out for her voyage to Antarctica. It was headed by Sir Ernest Shackleton who planned to cross the continent on foot from the Weddell Sea to the Ross Sea via the South Pole.

By January 1915 *Endurance* was gingerly picking her way through the Weddell Sea when pack-ice closed firmly round the ship and she was beset. Attempts to break her out with the engines failed: and after ten days Shackleton let his fires die out to save coal for heating instead of power. They were too far from land to sledge their stores across and huts were built on the floes alongside the ship for the expedition's 60 sledgedogs, which were exercised whenever possible. Seals were killed and stored to eke out the provisions and fend off scurvy and by the middle of March all hands settled down to their winter routine.

The *Endurance* drifted slowly northward.

In July changes to the ice became foreboding. Huge ridges appeared in the pack, forced up by heavy pressure. Over the next two months enormous masses of ice piled up in wild confusion. By October a renewal of heavy pressure started some of the ship's timbers, and she began to leak dangerously. Incessant hand-pumping kept the leaks in check; but there was no respite from the pressure, and by 26 October it was clear that *Endurance* was doomed. Shackleton ordered the three lifeboats, gear, provisions and sledges to be lowered on to the floes. A day later the rudderpost and stern-post were torn out, the decks cracked upwards, and the sea poured in through several gaping rents in the hull. Shackleton, the last man to leave the ship, looked down through the engine room skylight and saw the engines falling bodily sideways as their fixings gave way.

Twenty-eight men now found themselves hundreds of miles from all possible help, on drifting floes that would eventually break up. They had only a limited supply of food and fuel, and were exposed to the Antarctic winter.

Their best hope of survival was to reach Paulet Island, 350 miles to the north-west, where a hut, containing stores, had been erected for the Swedish Antarctic Expedition of 1902. The northerly drift of the floes would help them on their way; and when they reached the edge of the pack – or before, if it broke up – they would take to the boats.

On 8 April the floe the party was camped upon split in two, leaving the group on a floating triangular ice-raft. Next morning it split again – the crack running through Shackleton's own tent. The three small lifeboats – the *Dudley Docker*, *Stancomb Wills* and *James Caird*, each named after sponsors, were launched. Almost immediately they were nearly capsized in a furious tide-rip. Bailing furiously the party made for a safer-looking floe, and hauled the boats clear of danger.

But that night the new floe suddenly split and one man fell down the crack in his sleeping-bag. Shackleton gripped man and bag and pulled him back on to the floe. A few seconds later, the edges of the crack closed again with tremendous force. The 200 ft by 100 ft floe was surrounded by killer whales, sensing an imminent meal and blowing in the water all round the ice.

By mid-April they at last made solid ground and set up camp in an odiferous deserted penguin nursery on Elephant Island. They had only three months' food. The nearest help lay at Port Stanley, in the Falkland Islands, but this meant a beat of more than 500 miles against the prevailing north-westerly winds. South Georgia was 800 miles away but it was downwind. The risks of such a voyage, across the Southern Ocean, in a lightly-built, open boat were appalling. But there was no alternative and Shackleton was judicious in his choice of crew which included Frank Worsley, an intuitive navigator, Tim McCarthy, the ship's carpenter and Tom Crean, John Vincent and Harry McNeish, all tough sailors. The chosen boat was the *James Caird* – a 23 ft whaleboat which had a canoe stern. McCarthy decked her, as far as he was able, using ply-wood and frozen canvas, thawed out, foot by foot, on a blubber-fuelled stove. On 24 April sail was hoisted amid cheers from the shore and so began one of the greatest boat-voyages ever made.

Continually soaked from spray and leaks in the makeshift deck, shivering in the intense cold, the crew bailed out the water for the next 16 days as heavy winds and several gales battered the tiny hull. Worsley had to brace himself against the gunnels to get sunsights on his sextant and shouted the readings down to the men 'below'.

On the fifth day out a furious gale compelled the crew to heave-to. They used a sea-anchor to keep the boat dragging with her nose into the wind. When the winds abated they had to spend hours chipping off the ice which had coated the hull and rig. During one heavy gale Shackleton looked aft and saw a break in the cloudbase: a lighter coloured line running right across the horizon and believed the weather was moderating. But the 'clearing horizon' turned out to be a giant breaker which ran across the ocean as far as they could see. They survived the rogue wave, but on the eleventh day, just before midnight, they were almost overwhelmed by a colossal wave which left the boat half-full of water. 'During twenty-six years' experience,' wrote Shackleton, who was at the tiller, 'I have not encountered a wave so gigantic.'

On 6 May Worsley managed to get a sunsight which put the boat 100 miles from South Georgia. In two days they ought to sight it. If they missed it there was no hope for them or their comrades as they could never beat the *James Caird* back to the island.

Two days later, sure enough, signs of land began to appear: floating seaweed and cormorants and then the black cliffs of South Georgia came in sight at last. The party could not land that night; and next morning a violent north-westerly gale hit them. Setting what sail they could, they clawed desperately off the invisible, iron-bound coast. Next morning, 10 May, they at last reached, with great difficulty, the shelter of a tiny cove. All six were so weak that their efforts to haul the *James Caird* clear of the surf failed until food and rest had revived them.

After resting for three days they built up enough strength to take the *James Caird* to the head of King Haakon Bay. From here Shackleton and two of his men completed another incredible journey, crossing the snowy peaks of South Georgia to reach the Stromness whaling station. They took no sleeping-bags, had three days' food, a cooking stove, the carpenter's adze, for use as an ice-axe, and a 90ft rope. They extracted screws from the *James Caird*, and inserted them in the soles of their boots, as a substitute for crampons.

They stumbled into the whaling station and raised the alarm. A whaling steamer picked up McCarthy, Vincent, McNeish and the *James Caird*, while Shackleton set off in another steamer to rescue the rest of his men from Elephant Island. After many fruitless attempts he eventually picked them up on 30 August 1916. The men were preparing a lunch of boiled seal's backbone, limpets and seaweed. They had only four days' food in hand when they heard the report of a gun.

Shackleton's rescue of the *Endurance's* crew was seen by many as a greater feat than crossing to the South Pole. As for the stout little *James Caird*, she can be seen to this day in the Maritime Museum at Greenwich in London.

DECOY SHIP

U-boat commander Count Spiegel von Peckelsheim thought the old schooner in his gunsights, jogging across the Irish Sea was an easy target. She turned out to be a wolf in sheep's clothing

The three-masted topsail schooner *First Prize* dipped gently into the ocean swell as a light north-easterly breeze pushed her along at a leisurely two knots on passage from Milford Haven to Cork in Ireland on the evening of 30 April 1917. She was silhouetted against the setting sun, her red ensign fluttering innocently from the end of the mizzen gaff and she presented herself as the perfect target to Commander Count Spiegel von Peckelsheim, the German U-boat ace, who had already sunk 11 merchantmen since setting out from Emden earlier the same month. The aristocratic commander was on his way back to Germany with five prisoners of war on board U 93 and hoping to get there in time to watch two horses from his stables competing in the Berlin races.

A confident Spiegel invited his complete crew up on to the deck of the 200 ft long submarine which could motor at 15 knots on the surface, to show them just how quickly he could despatch an old schooner. She opened fire with her 4.1 inch gun at a range of three miles. The schooner luffed up into the wind to slow down and Spiegel watched as the ship's boat was launched to row away from the apparently crippled sailing ship. What Spiegel did not know was that the *Prize*'s 'skipper' was no civilian, but Lieutenant W. E. Sanders, of the Royal Naval Reserve and that the *Prize* was a sailing trap – a Q Ship – posing as a merchantman, but armed and reinforced with steel plate in critical areas. The launched ship's boat was not what it seemed either: far from being the complete crew rowing away from a sinking ship she was a 'panic party' designed to scull about maintaining a pose of shipwrecked mariners. Convinced the *Prize* had now been abandoned U 93 steamed in closer and opened up with his other gun – a 22 pounder – as well as the 4.1 gun and shelled the schooner, wrecking her engine, and wireless room, shredding her sails and injuring two hidden crew members. She started leaking and Spiegel, gaining confidence moved in for the coup de grace, but was careful to approach from dead astern where no guns could be trained on him, just in case the *Prize* was a Q Ship.

By doing so he fouled and carried away the schooner's towing log: a line with an impeller on the end which records the ship's distance run. Now convinced she was just another old coasting ship Spiegel ranged alongside the schooner's port quarter just 70 yards off her side. He now discovered the *Prize* wasn't quite what she appeared to be. Her red ensign suddenly came down and up instead went the White Ensign. She was no merchantman but a ship of the Royal Navy.

'Down screens! Open fire!' came the order as the forward deckhouse collapsed revealing a 12 pound gun and the main hatches over the hold opened to reveal another on a raised platform. A furious Spiegel fired two more rounds injuring another crew member and then desperately tried to ram the schooner, but found the listing hull was not within the turning circle of his steel fish so he altered course and tried to escape. Both guns of the *Prize* kept on firing until one shot blew the 4.1 inch gun to pieces, killing its crew. Another successful shot damaged the conning tower. In all 36 rounds landed on the surprised sub; her complete hull was glowing with fire down below and she appeared to sink stern first. But the *Prize* with her engine smashed could not manouvre over the stricken U 93 to finish her off with depth charges. So the 'panic party' picked up what they believed were the only three survivors which included Spiegel. All three were taken aboard the sinking *Prize*. In an ironic twist of fate Spiegel now discovered the schooner was in fact the first German 'prize' to have been taken by the Royal Navy in the 1914–18 War. The 112-foot long schooner had been called the *Else* registered at the German port of Leer, near the mouth of the River Ems. She had been captured in the western end of the English Channel and fitted out by the Admiralty as a decoy ship.

Spiegel now acted as a gentleman and promised to help nurse the limping Q Ship back to port. His navigating warrant officer dressed the wounds of the British crew and the German stoker petty officer, the third survivor, helped the schooner's mechanics to repair the engine and get it running again. Now through the nighttime hours the old schooner started heading for Ireland again. Two anxious days passed before she was taken in tow by a motor launch off the Old Head of Kinsale and hauled into Kinsale Harbour. Later a fishing drifter towed her back to Milford Haven. Spiegel and Sanders both believed U 93 had been lost. But although she was badly holed on the starboard side and unable to dive she had been nursed back to Germany making the long surface voyage, giving all shipping a wide berth, around the north coast of Scotland.

Just three months later the *Prize*, now disguised as a Swedish schooner, sailed back out into the Atlantic from the north of Ireland to resume her trap-ship duties. On 15 August she encountered UB 48 which torpedoed and sank her the following day.

DEATH DID NOT DETER HER

Her husband lost his mind and her ship was wrecked, but Ann Davison still went on to brave the Atlantic alone

In 1953, sailing *Felicity Ann*, a 23 ft double ended sloop, Ann Davison became the first woman to sail solo across the Atlantic. But although this lantern-jawed woman was the celebration of the maritime world, her feat was inspired by a much darker story.

It began in 1948 when Ann and husband Frank decided to run away from creditors. They had bought a 70 ft gaff-rigged fishing boat, *Reliance*, and spent several years fitting her out in Fleetwood, Lancashire. To pay for the work which needed to be done, they borrowed money and took out a mortgage: neither of which they could afford to repay. The plan was to use her as both a floating home and business: either chartering or fishing. When they received a notice of foreclosure, followed by a summons, they decided to flee and set sail for Cuba.

With very little sailing experience between them they were soon in trouble. Before they had left the Irish Sea a domestic paraffin stove which they had been using for cooking while moored safely in harbour, fell over while in use. It started a fire, which the pair had to fight with extinguishers and buckets of water. In the attempt Frank badly burned his hands.

Once out in the Western Approaches they were hit by a three-day gale, and tried running before it until finally giving up and riding to a sea anchor.

Next they had steering problems when the chain-drive from the wheel to the rudder head jumped off its cogs and jammed.

That sorted, they then noticed their masthead lamp had torn clear of its fixings and was being held aloft by the cable only. But they feared if they put into a British port a writ would be slapped on the vessel by their creditors.

With no idea where they were and with the engine playing up they were again hit by heavy weather. Suddenly one night the 'loom of a bluff like a blockhouse loomed ahead'.

In a panic Frank let the anchor go with 70 fathoms of chain and *Reliance* lurched round to the wind with a huge cliff beetling over her in the dark and the oppressive revolving flash of a lighthouse beam almost overhead.

In the morning a lifeboat turned up but was sent away by Frank who said they did not require assistance as though it was perfectly reasonable to anchor under the cliffs at Land's End. They lost their bower anchor as they tried to winch it in and once underway again were battered by continuing south-westerly gales blowing them on their way: but the wrong way, east up Channel instead of west and out into the Atlantic.

For a time Ann thought her husband had lost his mind: his eyes glazed over and he seemed to be hallucinating, believing the disarray down below from the rolling ship was the result of a fight, as they were driven ever onwards in the wrong direction.

For a short time they anchored – using the kedge anchor and the main halyard as a warp – off Plymouth, while Frank bailed out the rolling ship. Ann considered putting into port to get help for her husband. But she knew the legal miseries they faced would probably be worse for his state of mind. So they carried on westwards and then the wind dropped. Their sails flapped uselessly in the swell and a large ship signalled at them furiously to let them know they were drifting without lights in the shipping lanes.

When the wind picked up again they tried beating back out of the Channel, but finally under staysail and mizzen alone they closed Portland Bill at night, once more under the glaring beam of a powerful lighthouse.

Then *Reliance*'s jib carried away and in a rush to get the engine started they could get her firing only on one cylinder, which was not enough to clear the hissing seas of the Bill.

The boat was swept stern-first around the headland, pushed up the east side of the Bill and crashed ashore, snapping off her bowsprit and driving her bows straight in under the rocks.

Ann and Frank jumped into the black sea and clambered aboard their basic life-raft. They started paddling up along the coast towards Weymouth, but the set of the tide started to swing round again once they were a little further north of the Bill and carry them back out into the Channel. They were swept into the terrible Portland Race where Frank gave up the battle and died. Ann was swept around the west side of the Bill, and, now alone on the float paddled for her life onto a flat rocky ledge where she landed.

Ann and Frank had all along planned to start a new life on the far side of the Atlantic. It was an ambition Ann finally had to make solo. But when she got to the US the memory of her cavalier husband was not far from her thoughts.

BLIGH: A FLAWED REAL LIFE 'MASTER AND COMMANDER'

He was a great seaman but a poor man-manager. His vice was instrumental in his mutiny – his virtue the deliverance from it

Few of Fletcher Christian's cheering band of brothers can ever have expected to see their captain, William Bligh, again as they cast him adrift in a small open boat after the mutiny on the *Bounty* in 1789. They watched the 23 ft launch crammed with 18 men and with just eight inches of plank above the level of the Pacific Ocean drop astern without equipment, without shelter, without charts and almost without food.

But though Bligh's skills in diplomacy might have been lacking, his ability as a seaman and navigator were unsurpassed and he, along with 17 out of the original 18 castaways, spent 46 days at sea covering

4 254 miles from Tofua, in the Friendly Islands, to Timor, in the East Indies.

When a voyage to collect breadfruit plants from Tahiti and tranship them for re-planting on islands in the Caribbean was planned, Bligh was chosen as the man for the voyage. Having entered the Navy as an able seaman aged 16, Bligh had made his way up the ranks, without influence, by hard work and aptitude. It was his ability as a navigator and surveyor which won him the coveted post of sailing master aboard explorer James Cook's *Resolution* in the third of his famous voyages. And his conduct at the Battle of Copenhagen led Lord Nelson to summon him to the flagship and congratulate him personally.

Now Bligh had instructions to make for Tahiti by way of Cape Horn, load the breadfruit plants and take them to St Vincent and Jamaica.

For all his virtues, Bligh was dogged by an ill temper and a vicious tongue. He would not listen to anyone else's view and was good at rubbing people up the wrong way.

The *Bounty* sailed from Spithead on 23 December 1787 and after spending a month trying to bash round Cape Horn, Bligh gave up and used the prevailing westerlies to take him the long way round via the Cape of Good Hope, reaching Tahiti in October 1788. After their lengthy voyage and long stay loading the breadfruit, three sailors deserted for the charms of shore life in Tahiti, which included the friendly female population. They were later recaptured with difficulty.

At the start of the voyage home Bligh fell out with one of his officers, Fletcher Christian, who had grown to loathe life back aboard after the delights of Tahiti.

Christian seized the ship and offered all hands the choice of joining Bligh in the launch or remaining on board. Eighteen elected for the launch, and were supplied with a scanty stock of provisions, four cutlasses, a sextant and navigation tables.

The *Bounty's* launch, fitted with sail and oars, was designed to accommodate 13 men, not 19.

Bligh landed in Tofua, to obtain water, coconuts and breadfruit, but after four days the natives realised that without firearms the dreaded white men were at their mercy. Bligh saw that an attack was coming and put to sea under a shower of heavy stones which killed one of the party and wounded several others.

Bligh realised their nearest port of refuge was Timor, 4 000 miles away. He rationed each man to one ounce of biscuit and a pint of water a day and steered westward across the Pacific.

On the crests of long ocean combers the launch was in danger of broaching and capsizing, and in the troughs she lay almost becalmed. Only constant vigilance and top seamanship would keep her running before the wind.

On 4 May, when they had run something over 100 miles they sailed over a dangerous sunken reef, with only four feet of water covering it, and noticed they were among many islands, which Bligh charted. Four days later he had cleared the Fiji Islands.

Raw sea birds eked out the men's rations and regular rainfall slaked their thirst and they made good headway westward 100 miles and more a day. On 29 May they sailed through the Great Barrier Reef and landed on an uninhabited island about a mile off the coast of Queensland.

Here they repaired the launch – one of the rudder fixings had broken and it was simply luck that it had not sheared clean off. They gathered oysters and refreshed their water tanks and on 30 May, having named the place Restoration Island set off once more.

On the afternoon of 3 June they left the Australian coast and headed across the Timor Sea. Five days later they caught a small dolphin which helped with the victualling.

Finally on 13 June they anchored off the Dutch settlement of Kupang.

Of the men who had cast their captain adrift, most would probably have voted to put Fletcher Christian in the launch had they been able to read their fate.

In Tahiti, where most of the mutineers landed, one shot another dead after a row and was then himself stoned to death by his victim's native family.

Later on, the ship *HMS Pandora* arrived in Tahiti to collect the mutineers and bring them back to England to face a court martial. Of the 14 men taken aboard four were drowned when the ship was wrecked and when the remaining 10 reached Portsmouth aboard another ship, three were convicted of mutiny and hanged.

Other mutineers, including Fletcher Christian sailed on to the relatively unknown island of Pitcairn where the *Bounty* was burnt. Five of the men including Christian, were murdered by their Tahitian fellows in rows over discrimination.

Between the four who survived this further fatal arguments broke out after one of them invented a still and produced alcohol.

Of them all only one survived – John Adams – who was granted an amnesty in 1825.

DRIFTING ALONE ACROSS THE OCEAN IN A PUNCTURED LIFE-RAFT

Steven Callahan lost his boat when she hit a whale and crossed the Atlantic instead on a life-raft which he accidentally holed with a fish hook

Solo small boat adventurer Steven Callahan left Tenerife on 29 January 1984 on passage from the Canaries to Antigua aboard his home-built 21 ft cold-moulded wooden sloop, *Napoleon Solo*. Seven days out into the Atlantic about 800 miles west of the Canaries she hit an unidentified object – possibly a whale – at night and started to sink. Callahan deployed his six-man life-raft, *Rubber Ducky III*, made of circular rubber tubes with an internal diameter of 5 ft 6 ins under a canopy, and began a hellish journey that would end only after 76 days adrift. He deployed the sea anchor to stop the raft capsizing in the heavy seas and gale force winds that were blowing at the time his boat sank. But after two days he discovered two small holes in the flexing floor of the raft which he believed he made by sitting on his knife when he first clambered in. He then read the patching instructions which informed him the repair must be dry!

He used a cigarette lighter to try and dry the pinched up holes before applying glue, patches and Band-Aids.

He tore up a useless chart of the Indian Ocean, ripped it into ball-sized lumps which he then soaked and threw over the side measuring the time it took for them to drift away. He determined he was making about eight miles a day through the water. This, plus the current, gave him about 17 miles a day. At that rate, he reckoned it would take him 22 days to reach the shipping lanes: too long for his eight pints of water to last. So he hauled in the sea anchor.

He managed to get one of his solar stills to work which eked out his supply of fresh water and he used a spear gun – carefully wrapped in an old coat when not deployed – to catch fish.

On Day 14 Callahan saw a ship at night and fired six flares to attract attention. But she steamed by and he was not seen. A day later another passed by without seeing him. Then another. He had reached the shipping lanes.

When a wave knocked the raft down it filled with water soaking everything including his sleeping bag. He only knew such a wave was coming when the raft bent double and gripped him between its tubes before springing back to its normal shape.

On Day 40 Callahan realised with grim humour that this was the day his life-raft's guarantee ran out: 'If she fails me now do you suppose I *can* get my money back?' When his still suffered a leak in a seam which was near impossible to get at with a patch, he strapped a Tupperware box on the canopy of the raft to collect rain.

Forty-three days out disaster struck when a dorado fish fought the spear gun, snapped off the head of the spear then ripped a hole in the bottom tube of the raft with the broken spear tip. The air rushed out and *Rubber Ducky* sank down to her upper tube.

With just three inches of freeboard Callahan rolled the edges of the four-inch tear together to patch it with twine, tying the edges together around the patch.

He then reinflated the raft bringing the hole up out of the water, but 15 minutes later it had gone down again.

For two days Callahan battled to tie a better torniquet around the puckered hole. Sharks glided by as he was by now closer to the water. At last he managed to slow the air escape to 40 pumps every two hours. The sagging floor of the raft pinched Callahan's legs pulling the scabs off his salt water boils and adding to his misery.

Over the next eight days three more times the patch blew out and three more times Callahan had to refasten it using different sizes of line, and each time it required re-pumping. Meanwhile he fashioned a new spear-head for his gun out of a domestic table knife.

With the ingenuity of design brought about by desperation Callahan next used a domestic fork stabbed through each side of the tear and with codline behind it to hold it into place. Then he used a finer line to grip and pucker up the mouth of the hole over the stuffing through the hole. The codline and fork stopped the thinner line from rolling off.

Success!

The raft now only needed air added every 12 hours.

Using two pencils he constructed a makeshift 'sextant' and with the upper pencil in line with the Pole Star and the lower one in line with the horizon and the chart compass rose as a protractor he worked out a rough latitude. He was worried the north-westerly current would push him to the north of the string of Caribbean islands which arch away to the west above 19 degrees latitude. He hoped to keep drifting below 19 degrees to make land.

Sixty-one days out Callahan drifted through a Sargasso Sea of trash: plastic bottles, gobbets of tar, and fishing net, but within it were tiny crabs and shrimps which he ate by the mouthful.

Sixty-two days out his seventh ship passed by not noticing as he fired his last parachute flare.

He managed to grab a bird which landed on the canopy and after wringing its neck and skinning it, ate its breast meat.

As the colour of the ocean became lighter Callahan knew he was getting closer to shallower water.

On the night of the 75th day the bony sailor was overjoyed to see the loom of a lighthouse.

The next day he was picked up by an open fishing boat the *Clemence* and taken to its home port in Guadeloupe.

PART TWO

Calm

A SHIP SWALLOWED BY A CAVE

On her maiden voyage from Australia to London, the 179-foot tall ship *General Grant*, laden with gold bullion, was driven into a giant cave after becoming becalmed off a bleak, uninhabited island

Although the fog had lifted, a heavily overcast sky made the night of 13 May 1866 very dark. At around ten o'clock land was worryingly and unexpectedly sighted by an anxious William Loughlin, captain of the three-masted barque *General Grant*. She was nine days out of Melbourne, Australia, on the second half of her maiden voyage to London. On board were 33 crew, most of whom were British, and 50 passengers, including six women and 20 children. Some of the steerage passengers were emigrants returning home after years of gold-digging in the outback, with their earnings strapped around their waists in money belts. The ship herself was laden with £10 000 of gold bullion as well as a valuable freight of wool and hides.

After clearing Bass Strait, the stormy stretch of water between Australia and Tasmania, Captain William Loughlin shaped a course between the Snares, a cluster of rocks 50 miles south-west of Stewart Island, New Zealand and the Auckland Islands which lie 144 miles further south. This was a conventional route for sailing ships running down to Cape Horn and a safe course for any ship whose master was reasonably sure of his position.

But for those masters who allowed the fear of the Snares to play on their minds this reef was sometimes given too wide a berth. In the latter half of the nineteenth century at least 11 ships had been wrecked on the uninhabited shores of the Auckland Islands as a result of such over-correction.

There was only just enough breeze from the north-west to fill the heavy flax sails and maintain steerage way on the port tack aboard the Boston-registered *General Grant* and as land was sighted the over-cautious Captain William Loughlin realised he had sailed too far south. Now he made a second error of judgement. Perhaps it was wishful thinking, but Captain Loughlin ordered the ship to be run off before the fickle wind and steered south-east as he believed he was looking at the SW Cape of the Auckland Islands and such a course would sail him clear to the south. Soon, however, a much steeper, longer line of inhospitable cliffs loomed up ahead. The first land he had seen was Disappointment Island five miles off the north-west side of the Auckland Islands and not the SW Cape. Now the ship was steering straight for the Auckland Islands proper. All hands were called on deck to swing the yards and bring the *General Grant* round onto the starboard tack in a desperate bid to claw her off the land, but now what wind there was shifted to the west forcing the ship's head back towards the towering cliffs. All the time the giant ship was boxing about trying to fight her way off the land the prevailing east-going current was inexorably carrying her towards it and by now the boom of breakers could be clearly heard. The sound of the surf brought some of the passengers up on deck from their warm beds to ask questions of the harassed crew.

At around midnight the wind died completely leaving the ship rolling sluggishly in the swell with her sails slatting uselessly against the spars. In a hopeless gesture Captain Loughlin ordered soundings to be made with the ship's leadline, but no bottom was found. Even if it had been it was too late to rig out the anchors: it was seamanlike practice on ocean voyages to unshackle the ground tackle and lash it securely on the fo'c'sle head and store the anchor chains below: the last thing a skipper wanted was anchors slamming into the bow of the ship as she encountered huge seas off Cape Horn. To rig the anchors for use would take six hours.

An hour later the beetling cliffs were so close that the shouted orders on the deck of the *General Grant* echoed eerily back to haunt those giving them.

Captain Loughlin was reduced to pacing the deck whistling for wind while passengers and crew leaned on the bulwarks talking quietly and the stewards calmly prepared the ship's boats with provisions.

The oppressive silence was broken every now and then by the useless plopping of the leadline until the mate Bartholomew Brown, cried out: 'Ten fathoms'. As he did so a horrible splintering noise was heard as the jib-boom on the bow of the ship snapped off against a protruding crag. The 180 ft long *General Grant* recoiled from the impact and drifted stern first for half a mile until she smashed into another cliff edge, damaging her rudder and tearing off her spanker boom which crashed on deck fracturing two ribs of the crewman at the wheel. Now embayed by the two overhanging headlands, several hundred feet high, the ship having bounced off the cliff for the second time, had turned bow first towards the shore and drifted into a deep volcanic cave, which swallowed her completely as though she were a ship in a bottle.

Now the darkness became impenetrable and no-one on deck could see one end of the ship from the other. Passengers called out in fear of the unknown and were mocked by their echoing voices. As the ship drove further in her masts rubbed the roof of the cave dislodging earth and boulders which fell to the deck, killing and injuring several crew and passengers.

Captain Loughlin remained calm and ordered oil lamps to be lit and hung over the side. In the flickering gloom it was revealed that the ship was trapped in a huge vault of dripping, slime covered rock approximately 750 feet long, 150 feet wide and 180 feet high. Each time the swell welled into the cavern it drove the *General Grant* further in until she was constricted by the narrowing walls.

With five hours of darkness still to endure, Captain Loughlin ordered the ship's boats to be made ready for the dawn and loaded with small anchors in a bid to try and kedge the ship out of the cave. But until then the swell lifted the ship relentlessly until her foremast snapped in two and fell to the deck shortly followed by her mizzen topgallant mast which smashed through the poop deck injuring a number of passengers sheltering in the saloon.

As dawn approached the two ship's quarter boats were rowed out of the cave and the anchors dropped. They failed to get a purchase on the rocky bottom and when the lines were wound in on the capstans the anchors were pulled back aboard without moving the ship.

Now the wind, which had so cruelly let the ship founder, freshened and started pushing up a big sea. Captain Loughlin ordered the longboat to be launched, a lengthy procedure as she did not have her own davits but had special lifting gear which had to be rigged up prior to the long boat being lowered overboard.

While the gear was being prepared a large roller exploded in the cave lifting the ship by 10 feet jabbing her mainmast violently against the roof of the cave and breaking it in two. The ship's carpenter reported that water was filling the hold: the foot of the mast had dislodged planking on the bottom of the ship. At this the passengers panicked and clambered into the longboat while it was still sitting in its chocks. The special lifting gear was not required as the ship started to sink and as the maindeck became awash the longboat floated clear.

As the *General Grant* slid beneath the waves Captain Loughlin stood on the poop deck quietly awaiting the end with most of his crew.

Forty souls crowded the longboat of whom just six were sailors. They manned the oars and started rowing clear of the cavern but at the entrance to the cave the boat was swamped and capsized by a huge breaking wave.

The two remaining quarter boats picked up six survivors but now faced the daunting prospect of rowing six miles offshore to

Disappointment Island as the 30-mile-long cliffs of Auckland Island have no coves where a boat could be landed.

The 15 survivors of the ship's original complement of 83 spent two nights on the five square miles of Disappointment Island before taking the boats around to the east side of the Auckland Islands where they were able to find a bay and land. The Antarctic mid-winter was approaching and it was imperative they find food and shelter. Unlike the barren west side of the Auckland Islands which face the prevailing westerly storms and is bare rock, the east side is lush and verdant and here the survivors lit a fire, and lived off roasted seal meat. They built a hut with the timbers of other shipwrecked vessels and spent the next six months hunting for their food which included seal, albatross and mussels and making clothing from seal skins. Twice they sighted ships and lit huge fires to attract attention, but remained marooned. They made toy boats of scrapwood using the bladders of pigs and goats for buoyancy. Fitted with tin sails with the name of the ship, and the date she was wrecked carved on the model's 'deck', the boats were set adrift hoping someone would find them. Later, at a shack they found known as Musgrave's Hut, which had been constructed in 1864 by Captain Musgrave of the wrecked whaler *Grafton*, they found enough canvas to make a set of sails. These were fitted for one of the quarter boats, and the mate Bartholomew Brown and three other sailors set off for Stewart Island 200 miles away to get help. They departed on 22 January 1867 and were never seen again.

Finally on 21 November 1867 a whaling brig, the *Amherst*, anchored in the island's Port Ross cove and the ragged survivors rowed out to her in the remaining boat.

The nine men and one woman of the *General Grant*'s 83 passengers and crew were eventually landed at Bluff Harbour, New Zealand on 19 January 1868.

ORCHESTRA FROM HELL

Calm weather can offer a greater challenge to the lone yachtsman than the most frightening storm. Roger D Taylor composed a symphony from the cacophony of his drifting boat to stop himself going insane

Imagine climbing aboard a 20 ft junk-rigged, bilge keeler, lined out with carpet offcuts to protect against the sub-Arctic chill and stuffed full of instant mash potato, pre-cooked rice and squeezy Marmite and setting sail for Iceland. You have no engine, no EPIRB, no life-raft. You do have a sextant, GPS and handheld VHF.

Welcome to the world of minimalist sailor Roger D. Taylor and his gallant mini-steed *Mingming*, a customised Corribee Mark II, the cabin of which he has made even smaller by foam filling the ends behind watertight bulkheads—in case he hits an iceberg.

Roger is dismayed by many aspects of modern living: its shallowness, superficiality and spiritual death, and so, on voyages of soul therapy, pits himself against the great elements on plucky solo journies to the waters around Iceland and Greenland away from the land and towards the self. He confronts himself with a greater truth: how well has the science of his artifice performed, but much more importantly of what is he himself made?

En route his reverie of close-to whales, full on storms and sinister ice provide the Arthurian tests for hull and soul, but always the world he is escaping from intervenes: a centrally-heated cruise ship, a freighter with its website emblazoned in 60 ft letters, a deep-sea trawler dragging up the contents of the seabed . . .

But it is not always great winds that try this man, but great vacuums, too, when the wind dies:

> The wind had gone, but the sea seemed unaware and kept up its procession of steep-faced waves that threw us from one side to the other as they marched through, flinging the heavily battened junk sail this way and that, snapping the headsail back and forth in the little pockets of air that came and went with each advancing hillock, whacking the halyards against the mast. There is nothing calming about such a calm; it is a kind of torture, not simply of unrelieved and and random motion, but of maddening sound. *Mingming* is at her noisiest in such a calm. The rig and rigging and innards of the boat smash one way and then the other and the racket that goes along with all of this can by the third or fourth or fifth hour, drive you to distraction.
>
> Think of any onomatopoeic words you like:
>
> creak,hiss,bang.groan,whine,thud,ping,clang, for example. Then make up a few more:
>
> clipple,dink,sprug,kerlumph,pronk. Elide them all together and you just may start to capture a faint hint of the noise generated aboard a little junk-rigged yacht in a spiteful mid-ocean calm. Something like this: creakhissbang-groanwhinethudpingclangclippledinksprug
>
> Then without hesitation, it begins again, in a slightly transformed order:
> Hissthudclipplecreakdinkgroankerlumphwhinepronkclang
>
> Then the accents come in:
> dinkgroanTHUDhisskerlumphCREAKwhinePING
>
> Add some repetitions:
> kerlumphDINKDINKpingthudpronkPRONKcreakthud
>
> Then remember that this is often in two-part or three-part harmony, with endless lines of noise-based counterpoint running simultaneously:
> clangthudDINKsingsprugsprugcreakCLIPPLEgroanhiss
> creakPINGPINGclipplehissGROANthudTHUDclang
> angbanggroanCLANGclangdinkclipplethudpronkCREAK

As I lay there, hour after hour, drowned in this cacophonous nightmare, I began to curse my musical training. Long years of practice had habituated me to finding the rhythm and pitch and melody in every unlikely series of sounds. Instead of shutting out this diabolic symphony and letting me sleep peacefully, my wretched brain was constantly at work trying to analyse and notate the whole damn lot. To make things worse there was an easily discernible form and order to the seemingly random sounds. Wave motion is intensely rhythmic and it was wave motion that was powering every noise. The eerie repetitions and restatements generated a horribly logical counterpoint. Each squeak and groan had not just its own pitch but its own maddeningly clear tonality. Little notable tunes and phrases and fragments repeated themselves ad nauseam. Insane figures, stretti, little rondos, subjects, counter-subjects, developments, re-workings of a theme were hovering at the edge of recognition. Sonata form had nothing on the complexity of this infernal music. A thousand weird instrumentations suggested themselves. I could hear a D-major trumpet underpinned by bass clarinet. A barbershop quartet growled along in close harmony. An army of percussionists kept up a tireless improvisation. The dominant clacking themes, the banging and thudding and knocking, were overlaid with kaleidoscopic washes and suggested the unlikeliest of sound pictures: the whistling of a hundred hung-over milkmen, the baby bawlings of a metropolitan maternity unit, less distinct but most haunting of all, the death screams of some hellish abattoir. There was no limit to these wild juxtapositions. I tried to think of a composer who had attempted to capture this kind of incongruity. Ives, perhaps,Webern or Berg in pointillist mode, but it was no good – this quasi-musical pandemonium surpassed human invention.

In these conditions I sometimes capitulate and lower the mainsail lashing it down as firmly as I can to minimise any movement. The mainsail with its boom and battens and yard swinging and banging around the mast, is the principle source of all this noise. The mast itself locked between the partners and its step and passing just a foot or two from my head, serves as a tinny loudspeaker, relaying and amplifying the slightest whimper from above.

I lay down and tried to sleep but the symphonic racket tormented me. I stuffed plugs in my ears and buried my head under the blanket but there was no escaping it . . . I found myself sketching out in my head a snatch of ambient music. The full score would have 26 parts and last for about 37 hours without interval.

* * *

Extract from *MingMing and the Art of Minimal Ocean Sailing* by Roger D. Taylor, The Fitzroy Press, 2010.

DEATH AT THE HELM

Thanks to Richard McMullen and his solo sailing of heavy old boats in English waters, the world of small-boat sailors learned that it's safer to stay at sea in a blow than attempt to make harbour

It was a June evening in 1891, the wind was light and there was just a lazy swell running in the English Channel: easy conditions for the French fishermen who were working their nets off the coast of Normandy. It was almost midsummer and winds had been variable over the last few days, sometimes blowing from the west or south-west, other times from the north-east. It had been the latter direction which had scudded a 27 ft, six-ton lugger, the *Perseus*, down Channel from her mud-berth mooring at Greenhithe on the River Thames. The wind had been balanced well between her dipping lugsail, her jib and the small gaff mizzen and she sailed steadily westward. She must have appeared as just another fishing boat at first, although quite what an

English boat this size was doing so far from her own fishing ground was puzzling. Then the Frenchmen noticed she was towing a dinghy instead of nets. This was something none of them had seen before: a man sailing for pleasure. Without realising it they had just seen their first yacht. Intrigued, they took a closer look. A small, bearded man was sitting at her tiller and the fishermen gave a friendly wave. He did not respond. Then they noticed the boat was not making quite as steady a course as first perceived. She would luff up too far then bear away too far. They sailed nearer and noticed the bearded skipper was staring at the sky and that the tiller appeared to be moving his arm not the other way round.

The fishermen had come across the corpse of Richard Turrell McMullen who had died 24 hours before. McMullen, a London stockbroker, was a pioneer of small boat sailing who kept meticulous technical logs of the kit he used, the sailing qualities of his boats, the weather conditions he faced, and mistakes made. He noted the distances he sailed, the number of days or nights he spent on his cruises: some with his wife, some with paid hands, but mostly alone. He was to influence hundreds of readers and many followed him offshore.

He is credited with being the first sailor to emphasise that the worst danger faced by a small sailing vessel was trying to make harbour or anchorage in a blow: it was far better to get well offshore and ride out the storm in deep water.

This sage-like advice is first given in his book *Down Channel* when he sailed his 29 ft gaff cutter *Sirius* around Britain with two paid hands from Gravesend. We join him as he leaves Aberdeen with a single reef in the mainsail and the topsail lowered:

> Opening Girdleness the Sirius was borne over by a succession of terrific gusts from the south-east and encountered such a high breaking sea that I dared not put her on the course and bring the sea abeam. Though greatly overpowered, there was no alternative but to face it, until sufficient offing could be gained to enable the vessel to be hove-to and canvas reduced. Struck by one sea after another, the lads had to sling themselves into the rigging, and I had to let go the helm and cling with determination to the weather bulwark to escape being washed overboard. Momentarily expecting to be altogether disabled by a catastrophe to the spars, but compelled to go on, the situation until 8pm when we hove-to, was most critical. The boy was helplessly sick, and altogether

> useless, George, too, was sick, and I was expecting to be so. It blew a fierce gale on all the coast of Scotland that night. 10.30 pm, wind south-south-west, bore up under close reefs and ran before a great and hollow-looking sea.

At 3 am the following day he shook out three reefs and later passed through Kinnaird Roads off Fraserburgh, 'where eight schooners were lying-to under very short canvas, waiting as one of them informed me, for better weather.'

McMullen was handling the weather like the professionals: by remaining at sea rather than making a dash for harbour.

The body of R. T. McMullen was landed by the French fishermen at Beuzeval near Trouville. A doctor recorded the fact he had died of heart failure and been dead 24 hours when the fishermen found him. McMullen, aged 61, was buried in the local cemetery the following day after a simple service in the local Protestant church attended by his widow and brother.

SUNK BY A LEVIATHAN IN THICK FOG

Yachtsman Michael Dresden's 47 ft yacht was run down and sunk in Channel fog after a collision with a massive container ship

Michael Dresden, a 67-year-old retired solicitor from New Malden, Surrey and his four crew set sail in his £400 000 Moody 47 *Wahkuna* from the port of Dielette, in northern France bound for the River Hamble in Hampshire. It was May 2003, the weather conditions were good: wind variable Force 1 to 2, sea calm and the visibility was three to five miles. Once clear of the Channel Islands, a course was set for the Needles Fairway buoy, and the autopilot engaged. *Wahkuna* was making a speed of approximately 7.5 knots. Her position was plotted every 20 minutes by one of the crew. Halfway across the Channel and in the thick of the shipping lanes the visibility began to deteriorate and went down to 50 m. In addition to switching on the automatic fog signal, the skipper instructed the crew to raise the mainsail to increase their visibility both visually and by radar. The skipper and one other crew member were both constantly monitoring the radar which was set to the six-mile range, and they detected two ships, about a quarter of a mile apart, bearing approximately north-east at a range of six miles. The ships were visually tracked, until the range had decreased to three miles, when Mr Dresden assumed *Wahkuna* was on a collision course with the nearest vessel. He decided to take manual control of *Wahkuna* and slowed her down to under two knots. Later he still thought he was on a collision course and so he stopped the yacht altogether. He estimated the ship would pass ahead at a distance of 1.5 miles. Soon after one of the crew recalled hearing a fog signal, the bow of a large container vessel burst out of the fog steaming at 25 knots. Even had her captain wanted to it would take her two and a half miles to stop. 'The first 10 feet of *Wahkuna* was pulverised: it was like an explosion, it must have gone into particles,' Mr Dresden said. As a result of the impact, *Wahkuna* rose up two metres on the container vessel's bow wave and slalomed at an angle of 30° down her starboard side stern-first before being dropped back into the sea. The container vessel continued on her passage with *Wahkuna* scraping alongside. Moments later, the container vessel's stern passed, leaving *Wahkuna* in her wake. One of the crew managed to read the word Monrovia on the vessel's stern. Another recorded the GPS position. Mr Dresden could not send a Mayday by VHF because the mast, which housed the aerial, had been torn away during the impact. He then opened the forward cabin door to find water pouring in. Closing the door immediately, he instructed the crew to don lifejackets, and collect some food and water. He then put the main engine astern and began making stern way at a speed of about half a knot through the water. This reduced the water ingress, but it was soon realised that *Wahkuna* was sinking. Instructions were given to deploy and inflate the life-raft. After collecting flares and an EPIRB, the crew boarded the life-raft. Soon after, *Wahkuna* sank by the bow. Once in the life-raft, the crew tried to activate the EPIRB locating beacon, but the light indicating normal operation failed to illuminate. They were also unable to make any contact by mobile phone and therefore had to wait until they were seen by a passing ship. Some five and a half hours after boarding the life-raft, one of their flares was seen by *Condor Express*, a high-speed ferry operating between Poole, Weymouth and the Channel Islands. The crew were landed in Guernsey and taken to hospital for a routine medical examination. Later on that evening, they sailed to Poole on a return ferry.

Following enquiries by Ushant Traffic two Marine Accident Investigation Branch (MAIB) inspectors travelled to Hong Kong to interview the master of the ship who had reported seeing the yacht on his radar. During this visit, blue paint marks similar to *Wahkuna's* were found on the vessel's starboard bow.

P&O *Nedlloyd Vespucci* sailed from Antwerp on passage to Singapore. The following day she was travelling at 25 knots in thick fog when *Wahkuna* was detected on the port bow at a range of between five and six miles. By Automatic Radar Plotting Aid (ARPA), *Wahkuna's* course was northerly and her speed was 6.5 knots; the master estimated it would cross 8 cables ahead. However, when she was about one point on the port bow at a range of between 1.5 and 2 miles, *Wahkuna* slowed quickly and the ARPA vector indicated that she had also altered course towards the north-east. Then her speed by ARPA reduced to zero. This concerned the captain, who immediately started the second steering motor and ordered the second officer, who was then the Officer On Watch, to change to manual steering. This was done, but neither course nor speed was adjusted. The lookout on the port bridge wing did not see or hear anything, and the captain was completely unaware that a collision had occurred.

The MAIB concluded that actions by the ship and the yacht caused the collision.

They included the ship's excessive speed in such thick fog and the yacht crew's misinterpretation of the radar.

The MAIB found that commercial pressure might have influenced the *Vespucci's* captain in his decision to proceed at 25 knots in such conditions. Although the owners of the vessel denied such pressure is applied.

Mr Dresden, was a Yachtmaster and sailor with 41 years' experience and more than 120 Channel crossings under his lifebelt. He and his crew had crossed from Yarmouth to Cherbourg the previous Sunday, the Bank Holiday weekend, bad weather having delayed their departure by a day.

'Umpteen yachtsmen sail to France during the spring Bank Holiday: I totted up 37 ports on both sides of the Channel and the southern North Sea from which yachtsmen would, like as not, have been leaving. That ship must have been dodging yachts all day,' said Mr Dresden, whose insurers paid out in full just eight days after the accident.

'I am obviously very upset by the whole affair especially as my wife has had a big fright as well. I shouldn't really be here at all and now I'm not sure when I'm going to buy another boat, if ever. I lived for my sailing and having retired decided not to dally about but get on and have this lovely cruiser built while I had 10 to 15 years of active sailing left. Now I don't know what I've got left to live for.'

Perhaps the most chilling statistic which came out of the investigation was that produced by the Jobourg Vessel Traffic Service. On that fateful day they recorded by radar surveillance another 19 vessels in the vicinity at the time of the collision. Only one of them had reduced speed because of the fog.

THE SILENT CREEKS

Yacht designer, author and editor Maurice Griffiths had a marriage made in hell. His first wife Dulcie lived for deep keel yachts and the open sea, while her husband craved shoal draught boats and estuary creeks. After they divorced Maurice returned to his first love

As Stone Point came abeam and the Pye Sands stood between us and the seas coming round the Naze, the swell died down and nothing but wavelets remained.

Swan appeared relieved at the sudden change and the red buoy at the mouth of Walton Creek bubbled past, nodding his beweeded head as if to say "Oh, all right. Don't come up here if you don't want to." And the row of withies that stood against the edge of Horsey Island waved to us as though they themselves were surprised that any self-respecting yacht would prefer to go up Hamford Water for the night instead of the more congenial surroundings of the Twizzle and Walton itself.

The only beacon that remained neutral was the dear old thing with the can set jauntily on his head. I like that beacon. He is the one I usually run into when trying to make Walton Creek on a dark night. A canny withy indeed which has suffered much!

But tonight I wanted solitude. The Twizzle with its small crowd of yachts, the dinghies flitting here and there with vociferously happy crews; the congenial club house, with its crowded rooms and laughter and smoke-filled bar; the ladies room with its chattering occupants that seemed to all the world like a poultry run wherein a terrier has been let loose and the streets and 'prom' of the 'attractive watering place' itself. . .

No.

The sedge-covered flats of Horsey Island were slipping by close to windward and the lonely cries of wildfowl were carried across them by the dying breeze. Once a flock of redshank sailed across our bows on a level with the burgee, the swish of their wings passing like a gentle whisper in the trees. And Kirby Creek opened out, revealed itself abeam, then closed up once more and passed astern; just an opening in the sedge bank wherein one saw a twisting stream of water leading to – whence?

And Pewit Island to leeward with its deserted winding creek leading in towards the dim hills on the mainland past the quaint factory that seems almost derelict. There would by now be very little water and although with both plates and drop-rudder hauled up, *Swan* would float in twelve modest inches of moisture, down this narrow gulley the ebb was running fast emptying the expanse of shallow water that leads finally up to Beaumont's Quay.

On either side the mud was revealing itself in naked simplicity and a continuous hiss came from it as the tide receded: whilst here and there little jets of water spurted up where tiny creatures lived and throve.

The sun had just set behind vague clouds that had refused him one last look at the world before retiring for the night, and the darkness was waiting to descend upon us. The autumn air was chilly now and I beat my hands to restore their vanished circulation. Across a level bank of mud the trees on Skipper's Island were silhouetted against the darkening sky in the east. They stood clustered together as though afraid of the oncoming gloom, gaunt arms spread out towards one another, heads nodding sleepily, the grass at their feet already drowsy and inert. A faint air passed through their still branches and their sigh came delicately across the intervening mud and water, a sigh of contentment that a child makes when it is on the verge of Dreamland.

A gentle soft scraping brought me back to earth suddenly. The steel lug on the starboard lee plate was lifting. Pushing the helm down I grasped the tackle and hauled up the plate. For a moment *Swan* hung in stays tantalizingly then her tanned foresail filled again and with one sweep she had slewed round and was off towards the other bank pointing almost downstream. But in a minute she was again under proper control and beating lazily up against the ebb.

Once a number of fowl took to the air from the grass close to leeward and their sudden advent startled me as though a rifle bullet had passed through my mainsail.

As quickly as it narrowed, the creek opened out again and revealed a dim expanse of water on which ripples chased one another amongst tall grass that appeared here and there above the placid surface. It was now too dark to see the quay at the head of the creek, but one or two lights told where cottages that looked over the water, stood.

Hardly a sound broke the stillness of the night. The wind had almost died right away and only when a cat's paw kissed the tanned mainsail did the dinghy reveal its presence by murmuring contentedly. I looked back at my wake. It was smooth off the weather quarter and a line of bubbles was rising to the surface from under the rudder. We were making frightful leeway. Then she stopped. It was no use trying to get any nearer to the quay now. She was aground for the night. So was the dinghy. Never mind, it was quite a nice place and being a barge she would sit upright. I jumped over the side in my sea-boots and planted the anchor a few yards away. Then the canvas was stowed and everything on deck made shipshape.

It was quite dark now and while the Primus stoves were left to heat up a typical stew I sat on the cabin top and listened to the sounds of the night.

A train was pulling out from Frinton Station. A dog heard it and barked. A curlew from somewhere over Skipper's Island, called his mate and got no reply. Voices were coming from the direction of the quay and a motorhorn broke the stillness of the Kirby Road. And the mud all round was hissing as the last of the tide receded from sight, leaving a thin, tortuous rivulet that trickled down the middle of the creek a few feet from the yacht's bow.

The night grew colder as the stars appeared one by one and above the uncertain marshes, through which we had threaded our way, a mist was rising, ghostlike, unfolding its white coils over the damp grass and making the scene vaguer and more mysterious than ever.

It was eerie and lonely out here and somehow every sound ceased as though the rest of the world had suddenly been cut off and I instinctively pulled the collar of my jacket up and slipped my hands under the lapels. A dead, uncanny silence reigned over everything. And now the mist was around us, blotting out everything but the dark mass of the dinghy as it rested on the mud and the four yellow beams of light escaping through the portlights.

An owl hooted with startling suddenness from a far off spinney. The queer raucous voice rose to a hideous shriek . . . an unholy prophet of untold miseries . . . but I became aware of a slight odour. That stew had just begun to 'catch'.

But what a change next morning! The early sun, glad to be about again was glinting on the dew covered deck and what had been the previous night murky stretches of uncertain mud was now an expanse of mirror-like water. Hardly a breath stirred and the reflections of the trees were reproduced faithfully on the placid surface. From the wharf a barge was drifting down, light, her familiar topsail and big mainsail set in the hope of catching any draught that was going. It was just high water and the islands that had last night appeared as high banks of mud with gaunt sedge on the top now seemed to be flat fields of coarse grass out of which grew lonely rotten stumps and broken withies. The barge drifted nearer, her reflection playing idly before the bluff bows, and her dinghy following on the end of a heavy painter that drooped in the middle to the surface. As the stately old vessel glided past within a few yards of *Swan*, the old skipper left the wheel and stood against the rail, hands in pockets, surveying the unfamiliar little barge yacht.

'Nice mornin''

I agreed and begged to ask his opinion on the chance of getting any wind today.

'Aw, yus. Nice breeze'll come up from th' southward later on.'

I thanked him and watched his little white terrier pacing the deck at twenty-five miles an hour.

And when they had gone and only the masts and patch tanned sails appeared over the sedge grass of the unnamed islet. I stripped in the well, paused for a deep breath on the cabin-top and then dived into the limpid depths of the creek. And everywhere silence reigned, the silence of big open spaces, of nature at her best, of the – creeks.

* * *

This is an extract from *The Magic of the Swatchways*, by Maurice Griffiths, published by Adlard Coles Nautical, 2000.

PART THREE

Storm

FASTNET 79: THE KILLER STORM

Twenty-one yachtsmen drowned when a Force 10 storm ripped through the 306 yachts competing in the 1979 Fastnet Race

The wind began its life in the treeless Great Plains of North America where the summer heat, reflected by an ocean of white corn, shimmered skywards becoming turbo-charged with colder air sucked in from Canada to fill the void. The twister soon left the waving ears of wheat behind to dump a deluge of rain on Minneapolis before powering itself into a 60-knot tornado which ripped off roofs, downed power lines and tore off tree branches, one of which killed a woman walking in New York's Central Park.

The angry, swirling, black, cornet-shaped sky, left terra firma over Halifax, Nova Scotia, and headed east across the Atlantic just as 2 700 sailors in 306 yachts crossed the start line off Cowes in the

Isle of Wight heading for the Fastnet Rock, off south-east Ireland, the rounding point for the 605-mile Fastnet Race.

Three days later 21 yachtsmen were dead: 15 of them competitors in the Fastnet Race and six from two other yachts in the storm's path.

The worst hit yacht in the Fastnet Race was *Ariadne*, a Carter 35, from West Mersea, Essex, sailed by her American owner Frank Ferris, 61, and his five-strong crew. Two days into the race, gale force winds split the yacht's reefed mainsail and *Ariadne* was reduced to a reefed number three jib, but was still in the race. At midnight after the crew heard the shipping forecast which predicted the wind increasing to Force 10, they retired and ran off before the wind. They replaced the number three jib with a smaller one and finally took that down too and set up a tiny storm jib. Two hours later the storm jib blew into ribbons and was deliberately towed over the stern to try and slow the boat down. A while later the boat was rolled over completely by a huge breaking wave. One crewman was thrown overboard, but thanks to his harness was able to scramble back onto the boat. Another crewman, Bill LeFevre, had been seriously injured and the boat dismasted. The boat's washboards – which act like a cabin door – had been smashed in and she was half full of water. The crew started bailing out the water with buckets and saucepans. As dawn lit up the 40-foot waves, *Ariadne* was rolled again throwing two crew into the sea. David Crisp was hauled back aboard by his harness, but Bob Robie's harness failed and he was seen waving 50 yards away before disappearing into the trough of a wave and never seen again.

Ferris now decided to abandon ship and the five men climbed into the life-raft and drifted away from the half-filled hull of *Ariadne*. After two hours they spotted a German freighter, the *Nanna*, but before the ship could reach them the raft, too, capsized. During the difficult task of clambering up the rolling ship's ladder, Ferris either misjudged his moment or was hit by the side of the ship and was washed away and lost. Matthew Hunt successfully leapt from the upside down raft onto the ladder and scrambled for safety. Then to his horror noticed that David Crisp, who had also successfully made the ladder was still attached to the life-raft by his harness. As the ship rolled he was yanked off the ladder by his harness and both he and the badly injured Bill LeFevre were swept under the ship's stern.

Matthew Hunt and Rob Gilders, who had also managed to scale the ship's ladder, were the only two to survive from *Ariadne's* crew of six.

Meanwhile the rescue of other yachtsmen was continuing with five lifeboats, seven helicopters, three Nimrod aircraft, tugs, trawlers, and tankers, Royal Navy ships and ships from both the Dutch and Irish navies.

Five boats sank, 100 were knocked down, dipping their masts in the water, and at least 75 were rolled right over, most of them losing their masts in the process. Many boats also had their flimsy rudders snapped off by the gigantic seas.

Among the boats successfully recovered and towed back to shore was *Ariadne*.

A CHOP-STICK FORTUNE IN THE SOUTH SEAS

Many men have sought their fortune in far away places. Weston Martyr was no different, but a typhoon put paid to his get-rich-quick plans in the South Pacific

A century ago when the world was a bigger place than it is today and much of it coloured pink from the sprawling territory of the British Empire, it was not uncommon to find young Englishmen in far away places – where the atlas wasn't pink – looking for adventure and fortune. One such was Weston Martyr, who had been at sea in square-riggers, and had found himself penniless in the exotic Chinese port of Shanghai where he signed on as able seaman aboard a schooner, named the *Chichishima Maru*, registered in the Japanese port of Uraga. Her skipper was Sam Payne who Martyr described as a 'good and loyal friend, but whose trouble was whisky and women and being born too late. He would have made a first-class Elizabethan'.

Payne had a money-making scheme: to sail to an atoll in the German-controlled Caroline Islands in the western Pacific and dive for trochu snails, the shells from which were used in the manufacture of mother of pearl necklaces and buttons. Payne had reckoned one voyage would make £6 000 as the Japanese were paying 800 yen a ton at the time.

One small problem was that the German administration had put a preservation order on the reef and in any case fishing in their territory was forbidden without a permit. This meant the trochu were thriving in great numbers and Payne needed some hard cash. He had told Martyr that the atoll would provide fresh water if they dug a well, and there was fish in the lagoon, and coconuts ashore for victuals. The pair formed a partnership and signed on four Chinamen as crew, including a cook.

It was a hard slog mostly to windward: not the best point of sail for a schooner, but eventually the *Chichishima* dropped anchor in the lagoon of the uninhabited atoll which was less than a mile in length and a third of a mile wide. It highest peak rose no more than eight feet above the high water mark. It consisted of sand and the stumps of coconut palms: ominously a recent typhoon had stripped the atoll bare.

After a four day digging expedition revealed no more than one bucket of brackish salt water, they gave up on the well and started rationing their 400 gallons of fresh water aboard the schooner. The trochu shells had to be plucked by hand off the reef then laid out in the sun so that the snail occupant was left to rot and dry out.

Payne made a box with a glass bottom in order to survey the reef and find the snails for which the schooner's four hands would dive. When the plan was explained – with difficulty to the non-English speaking hands – the cook revealed that none of them could swim. This floored Payne who went below for a stiff drink, meanwhile the Chinese cook, who understood enough English to know that all the crew were on a share of the fortune to be salvaged, came up with a simple plan. From the ship's dinghy and using two long bamboo poles in the manner of his national cutlery he picked up the shells from the sea-bed as another Chinaman used the glass-bottomed mask to guide him to the unsuspecting snail.

The crew set to and made two more sets of giant chop-sticks, hinged with iron bolts and weighted at the bottom end with ingots of melted lead ballast. Armed with two more DIY glass-bottomed masks, the crew of the *Chichishima* had 3 000 snails drying out on the atoll beach after their first 12 hours labour.

After the first week's 'production' 28 000 snails lay rotting on the beach. After six weeks of work they had 120 000 shells rotting on the beach waiting to be loaded onto the schooner as soon as the smell was bearable.

And then the glass started to fall and the wind started to freshen up. The crew put out another anchor and also ran a huge warp ashore and made it fast to a clump of palm tree stumps. The following night a typhoon hit them and in the gusts the schooner lay over under bare poles with the edge of her deck in the water.

Daybreak revealed mountainous seas exploding on the windward side of the atoll and sweeping right across the beach into the lagoon. When the wind died the crew went ashore.

Every single trochu shell had been washed back into the sea!

FATAL DELIVERY TRIP

British Prime Minister Edward Heath lost his godson when a storm wrecked his racing boat

It had been a bad year for Edward Heath and it was about to become a disastrous one. The Conservative Party leader had lost the General Election in February 1974 and in August that year, racing his third *Morning Cloud* at Burnham Week, the yachting politician did not win a single trophy for the first time in five years at the Essex meet. But that was nothing compared to what was now about to happen.

As the week ended Heath flew off from Southend Airport to Ostend in Belgium for a reunion with his old wartime regiment. Before he left he arranged a delivery crew to sail his 45 ft sloop from Burnham-on-Crouch to Cowes in preparation for the following weekend's racing on the Solent.

The skipper was Don Blewett and among the crew was Heath's godson, Christopher Chadd. By the time they got out of the river the strong south-westerly wind which had sped them down the Crouch was bang on the nose as they came into the West Swin Channel. For a time they beat against it, but then Blewett changed his mind and decided to run off north, and clear the treacherous Thames Estuary sands to starboard. It was a longer route but he would have a beam wind for the next leg past the North Foreland.

They had a rough trip across the estuary and the seas off the North Foreland were considerable: and this was in the lee of England. Once through the Downs they would be facing the full force of the gale and Blewett did consider putting into Dover to wait for the wind to ease up. Heath himself, thought his 'movement crew', as he called the non-racing crew, would run for shelter to either Ramsgate or Dover should there be any doubts over the weather.

It's easy to convince yourself that conditions have improved once you get some shelter under a weather shore, which is what *Morning Cloud* enjoyed as she surged along off East Kent, with Heath's birthplace at Broadstairs clearly visible to her crew off the starboard side.

But even so conditions did seem to have improved as she reached Dover and the delivery crew decided to press on. The following day however the winds increased and late that night rounding the Royal Sovereign light vessel they recorded gusts of 45 to 50 knots with huge seas piling up. *Morning Cloud* was now under heavily-reefed mainsail alone and, although she was making up to five knots through the water, was making little headway over the ground against the foul tide. When the next ebb eventually gave them a lift it also increased the already big seas as the Channel started moving bodily against the gale. *Morning Cloud's* flush decks offered no shelter to the exhausted crew, but their morale improved when they picked up the flash of the Owers light: not too far beyond that lay the shelter of the Isle of Wight.

That night as Heath listened to the news of the rough weather he hoped his movement crew were either through it and into the Solent or sheltering in Dover.

When *Morning Cloud* was launched at Clare Lallow's Cowes yard in April 1973 the wife of one of Heath's crew members lost her balance in the crush of onlookers and fell from the sea wall to the concrete slipway below and was taken to hospital suffering from concussion. Heath overheard someone say: 'This will be an unlucky boat.'

Just over six miles east of the Owers light *Morning Cloud* was knocked down and two crew went overboard. One was hauled back by his safety line, the second, Nigel Cumming, was missing: the torn end of his harness trailing over the side. The boat was immediately put about but the search was hopeless and they resumed their course for the Solent. *Morning Cloud* was then thrown over again putting her mast underwater. This time Christopher Chadd, who was just coming into the exposed cockpit from the companionway, and before he had time to clip on, was swept overboard.

The crew had one glimpse of him before he was swept away.

Now Blewett discovered some deck beams had cracked and water was coming into the hull's three skins of mahogany, which had suffered structural damage. The forehatch was also missing: either ripped off by the seas or blown off from the pressure of air as the wave which swept Chadd away entered the boat. Sea water had ruined the VHF radio.

Blewett decided to abandon ship and launched the four-man life-raft. A bigger life-raft, able to hold six men, and the locker lid which protected it had been swept clean away. The five remaining crew, two with injuries to ribs and shoulder blades, clambered into the overcrowded life-raft and let her drift on a drogue.

They only managed to let off one flare – which was immediately blown flat – before the others were soaked and would not ignite.

The gale blew the life-raft back up the coast and eight hours later they were tipped into the breaking surf on the shingle of Brighton beach.

Some days later the wreck of *Morning Cloud* was lifted out of the water at Shoreham. It was a shocking sight. The whole of her starboard side, deck and keel had been torn out. She looked like a half model.

When Heath put to sea again in *Morning Cloud IV* he had his crew fitted with lifelines which were double the recommended strength.

ANCHORING A TALL SHIP IN A PUDDLE

Sailing a small boat in narrow waters during an onshore gale is a nerve-wracking experience. Imagine doing the same thing in a tall ship

Even today yachtsmen are wary of the sand-muzzled entrance to the River Elbe in Germany which is the watery highway to Hamburg. The shoal banks are always shifting, the river is busy with huge container ships and, worst of all, it faces the weather. Unlike the much wider Thames Estuary on the opposite side of the North Sea, which has England in the way of prevailing westerlies, the Elbe's low-lying mouth faces the open sea.

So if small boat sailors take great care when navigating the Elbe estuary, imagine what it must have been like one night in late December 1909 when the 3 000-ton, four-masted barque *Pitlochry*, deep-laden with 4 000 tons of nitrates – used as agricultural fertiliser – was approaching in a Force 10 blizzard. Her captain, Robert Miethe, one of the old time skippers, hugely respected by both his crew and his employers, had made another fast passage home from Tocopilla, Chile. His 63 days at sea had beaten the much bigger, five-masted barque, *Preussen*, favourite of the Kaiser, by 11 days.

But Miethe was a victim of his own success. His smart use of the weather systems, after rounding Cape Horn, had found him the trade winds in the South Atlantic early, and by the time he was in the Western Approaches a Force 8 gale sped him up the English Channel in mid-channel to avoid coastal hazards, but with no time to signal any coastguard stations as to his presence.

Off Terschelling, one of the Dutch Frisian islands, the wind died completely. The glass – which had been dropping steadily as the depression which sped *Pitlochry* up Channel, swirled away eastward – stopped. Miethe noticed how near the sandy coastline looked, how sharp it was delineated. He knew he was in the middle of the weather system and the cold front would soon be upon him bringing its veering wind system.

But for now the ship just wallowed in an eerie, foreboding swell: her sails slatted against her masts, her chain sheets rattled on their horses and the crew paced nervously up and down the deck.

Miethe noticed that the normally busy North Sea was deserted: not even an inshore fishing boat could be seen. More importantly for him there was no sign of a pilot boat. In the back of his mind he knew storm signals would be flying at all the harbour-mouths in the vicinity.

Then his ship was hit by a blast of hail. Sails were reefed as a gale sprang out of nowhere, and the crew burned blue flares: the signal for the pilot. But Miethe had made such a fast passage that the ship's office staff were not expecting him and no pilot had been sent out.

Now the wind increased from the north-west and the *Pitlochry* was embayed in the Heligoland Bight: pinned into the shallow corner of the North Sea where Germany nudges Denmark. Handy vessel though she was, no ship could tack in a Force 10, gusting 11, onshore wind and she did not have enough sea room for Miethe to wear ship either: gybing round would drive her downwind onto the shoals where she would be wrecked, before she could make sufficient offing.

Miethe had no choice but to sail up the river himself, without a pilot.

Now, in the darkness, with hail stones raining down and the wind at hurricane force, the bold captain had his mate standby on the fo'c'sle head with a club hammer ready to knock out the anchor stops. His carpenter and blacksmith were also standing by the windlass brakes to ease the chain out. If they let it go with a run it would pull straight out of the ship, if they braked too hard the snubbing action could part the cable.

As he picked up the first of the Elbe lightships, *Pitlochry's* main lower topsail blew clean out of its boltropes: 'Away blew the great sail toward Cuxhaven to let them know we were coming,' said Miethe, later.

The winking lights of the channel buoys swayed in the storm as *Pitlochry* – now with the flood tide under her as well – charged into the river at 18 knots. Two more light vessels passed by flashing their warning lights. Then the ship was blasted by sand mixed with the hail as the howling wind tore across the uncovered shoals either side of the channel.

Miethe knew he had only one chance: as soon as he had the Elbe No 5 light vessel abeam he would have to bring his ship round into the wind and drop both anchors. Any further up the river and he would find no room to bring up: there would be too many ships.

He took in more sail and as the Elbe No 5 approached he saw the dark river come alive with speckled anchor lights. Many were steamers riding to anchors but with their propellers turning to take some strain off their cables as they desperately tried to stay on station.

He had to find room in among them as the Mittelrug Sand was close and if *Pitlochry* hit that she would break up immediately. For the first time in her long passage all crew were in lifejackets just in case of this very scenario.

Miethe brought her round to starboard and as the ship stalled and 'stood upon her wake' the order was given to let go.

Both anchors roared away, the chains jumping clean off their drums and the hawse pipes spitting out sparks in the dark as 150 fathoms on both hooks gunned over the side. The windlass men carefully surged the brakes and the ship with her cables standing out like 'twisted violin strings' came to a halt with just six feet under her keel and 50 yards from the Mittelrug Sand.

The next morning the pilot could not believe his eyes.

As for Miethe he found an extra 2 000 marks in his bank account a day later.

THREE TIMES CAPSIZED SAILING ROUND ANTARCTICA

A bold bid to become the first solo sailor to circumnavigate Antarctica failed for David Lewis but his voyages are still celebrated among sailors the world over

Ocean sailor and Polynesian scholar David Lewis, made a brave bid to become the first yachtsman to sail solo around Antarctica. But the feat almost cost the East End doctor his life. He capsized his 32 ft steel yacht, *Ice Bird*, three times and was dismasted twice. He left Sydney, Australia in October 1972 and six weeks later was barrelling over huge seas when he was knocked down. Lewis found his self-steering unit had been torn off and his headsail split. He took all sail down and locked himself below trying to steer the boat with internal tiller lines in a desperate attempt to keep her running before the wind under bare poles. Two weeks later as the wind rose to hurricane Force 13, the 70 mph storm turned the whole seascape white and *Ice Bird* was smashed down again from a huge breaker which rolled her through 360 degrees. This time her mast was ripped off, the forehatch plucked from the deck and the life-raft tossed away in the maelstrom. *Ice Bird* was now full of water. Lewis bailed for his life for the next 10 hours until the wind 'dropped' to a Force 9–10.

A day or so later he rigged up a jury mast with variously a spinnaker pole and the yacht's boom, set a storm jib on it and headed for the 'shelter' he hoped he might find on the Antarctic Peninsula which was 2 500 miles away.

After eight weeks a frost-bitten and exhausted Lewis nosed *Ice Bird* into a world of snow-covered land as she limped into Palmer Antarctic Station on Anvers Island. The American scientists based at the Palmer station provided Lewis with medical assistance, a warm bed, fresh clothes, and help in re-designing *Ice Bird*'s sloop rig into a gunter-rigged craft with the old broken spars.

It was the spring of 1973 before Lewis set off again. While under power *Ice Bird* was almost battered to pieces in a huge swell which was washing small icebergs against one another and he almost did not have enough power to navigate through. After making headway through a few leads in the ice he was eventually beset: jammed in the frozen sea.

When he eventually managed to break free he soon discovered *Ice Bird*'s gaff was too unwieldy a spar for a solo sailor and he dispensed with it and rigged the reefed mainsail back on the stumpy mast as a cut-down Bermudan rig.

Next he was plagued by two weeks of fog in which *Ice Bird* drifted blindly while Lewis listened to the terrifying crash of the ocean swell on the waterline of unseen icebergs.

Then six weeks out from Antarctica he found himself in the eye of a hurricane: the sudden calm was eerie and the combers – without the wind to flatten them – were now leaping up in watery triangles. Following his two earlier capsizes, Lewis was by now understandably terrified of heavy weather and as the glass rose, Lewis's spirits dropped and he was hit by the cold front which came out of nowhere at 50 knots, quickly building to 80 before his wind instruments broke.

Ice Bird was now surfing down 40-foot waves which were 'tumbling into surf'.

One of these monsters lifted *Ice Bird*, smashed her down on her side into the trough and rolled her completely over: her third capsize of the voyage. She was also dismasted once more.

Fighting off feelings of despair, Lewis made another jury rig this time a spritsail rig using an old sweep as the sprit.

The bid to circumnavigate Antarctica was well and truly over. Three weeks later *Ice Bird* arrived in Cape Town.

Lewis made his sailing name in the first OSTAR – single-handed transatlantic race – in 1960, when he finished third in his 25 ft yacht after being . . . dismasted.

PART FOUR

Human Error

UK BORDER PATROL OF YESTERYEAR

During World War Two the Royal Navy insisted UK sailing ships anchor at night to stop them being mistaken for enemy craft. This caused much ill feeling from skippers losing a fair wind or tide. So when barge skipper Bob Roberts got the chance to get his own back revenge was sweet

Britain's last sailing ship captain Bob Roberts was skipper of the Thames barge *Cambria* and in 1970 carried the last freight under canvas: 100 tons of cattle feed to Ipswich, Suffolk from Tilbury Dock. Bob was a man whom history chased. His whole life at sea was in sail, but each time he got a new berth it was in a craft shortly to become obsolete. We join him aboard the *Martinet*, the last of the boomie barges, to hear his hilarious story about the naval patrols which guarded the UK's Home Waters during World War II making sure no enemy craft threatened the British coastline.

The night after leaving Ipswich we anchored near the Ridge buoy in the entrance to the River Crouch. It was a safe, snug berth and we intended to be off up-Swin to London in the early morning.

The sails having been stowed and everything made shipshape on deck, Jerry and I retired below with a pair of nicely edged appetites for our usual evening meal – a sort of high tea taken rather late but not quite late enough to be called supper. We made a practice of it for years and it suited us during wartime when the regulations compelled us to anchor during the hours of darkness. If the weather was at all reasonable we could say that the day's work was done and sit down in peace and comfort.

Just before we ranged alongside the cabin table we heard the noise of a motor boat and went on deck again in answer to a rather faint-hearted hail. It was a small patrol boat, obviously manned by amateurs. Her skipper wanted to know the usual details, 'where from, where bound, etc' and I told him. He then chootled off up-river towards Shore-Ends.

Thinking we had seen the last of him and having no other cares we fell-to upon fried sausages, onions and mash, swilled down with great mugs of tea and followed by a pipe of tobacco and a musical programme on the wireless. We had shut the cabin door, and the fire, drawn up by the easterly wind, glowed cheerfully.

We were enjoying these simple luxuries without the slightest notion of what was going on outside until the mate said he thought he heard that motor boat again. We turned off the wireless and sure enough we could hear the propeller churning the water near us. Noises in the water are very distinct when below decks. I went up the stairs to investigate.

At the doorway of the deckhouse which led to the companion I met with a horrible shock. I found myself staring at the end of a machine gun, pointed threateningly at me from the deck of the motor boat by a dim figure who seemed to be in an awful temper. He was saying 'I'll show them. I'll show them. I'll make them answer.'

My life was saved by someone in the stern of the boat shouting in a voice full of alarm:

'Don't shoot, skipper. Don't shoot. There's someone standing there.'

That was me.

'Why didn't you answer my hail?' demanded the skipper haughtily.

'I didn't hear you,' I said. 'You should learn to shout.'

I knew that most of those lads were not well versed in seamen's ways. When a seaman wants to hail someone or get aboard his ship he learns, through experience, that he can cool his heels for many a long hour unless he kicks up an unholy hullaballoo. This he does, whistling, shouting, and making far-reaching noises, interspersed with the name of the ship required, so that he can be heard for miles around and often in the next county.

But these newcomers to sea-life would cruise around muttering 'I say' and expecting us to take notice of them. I had been approached by such faint mumblings before and I immediately suspected that these people in the patrol boat had failed to make full use of their lungs.

However, the skipper was furious. He had felt insulted at not being answered promptly, had threatened to fire on the *Martinet* in a fit of temper, and was not in the least calmed by my eventual reply.

I saw no reason for all this, as we had previously given him our details, and told him so. I felt not a little nettled that I might have had my body riddled with bullets by this idiot had not the other fellow seen me and spoken up in time.

That danger having now passed I took every opportunity to pour scorn and sarcasm upon the officer in charge as a sort of revenge for his high-handedness. He demanded to know what cargo we were carrying. We had none, being light and high up out of the water. Any seaman with half an eye could have seen that the *Martinet* was empty.

'Did you ever see a loaded barge standing up out of the water like a church?' I jibed. 'Can't you see we're only drawing three feet forward? Shine your torch there and have a look. Why can't you use a bit of common sense, you blank so-and-so?'

All this drove the patrol skipper nearly crazy.

'I'm sending an armed party. Lower a ladder at once,' he shouted angrily.

'What do you think we are?' I answered. 'The Queen Mary? We haven't got a ladder and if we had I wouldn't lower it. If anyone wants to board this barge they can damn well climb up the side the same as we have to.'

I suggested that he bring his motor-boat alongside, for there was a strong spring ebb running. But it looked as though he did not know how to set about doing that, for he ordered two hands away in a tiny dinghy only about ten feet long.

To begin with they had a dreadful frap-up through one man unhooking the forward davit tackle while the after one was still fast. As the motor-boat was going slow ahead all the time to stem the tide, the bow of the dinghy swung round and its occupants were being towed stern-first in an exceedingly dangerous fashion. The painter had not been made fast and the stern was hanging half out of the water, suspended by the after tackle.

Jerry and I sat on the hatches and passed remarks and offered hints which were not appreciated. Neither were all these remarks in the best of taste. But it was the only way we could get our own back on this imperious officer.

When at last the two men in the dinghy got it adrift they were carried downstream from the *Martinet*, and it did not seem to occur to their superior to tow them up slightly ahead of the barge so that they could sheer over to us with the tide. They set to and rowed vigorously with two rather small paddles, hindered somewhat by the fact that they wore heavy coats and were cluttered up with rifles and ammunition to enforce their authority when they reached the *Martinet*.

They rowed and they rowed and they rowed. As the tide swept them astern of us they quickened their strokes to an almost frantic pace. Both men were on the big side and they presented, to us, a very funny spectacle in so small a dinghy.

The officer aboard the motor boat did nothing to help them. He just strutted up and down his miniature deck, obviously fuming and perhaps wondering why his men took so long to row over to us.

At last the armed party, on the point of exhaustion, got to within about fifteen yards of us and out of sheer sympathy for their plight we floated a heaving line down to them and hauled their cockleshell alongside. They had no idea how to get aboard an empty, high-sided barge, and in any case their arms and backs must have ached too much to heave their heavy bodies up. Rather hastily, they both gripped the covering board and clung there, hanging on by their finger tips. The dinghy drifted from under them and for a moment I thought they were going to lose their grip and drown.

Jerry and 1 leaned over the rail and grasped them by the shoulders but could not pull them up until we had relieved them of their rifles, which we threw on to the hatches. We then hove the men up, hand over hand, by the back of their coats, coming eventually to the seats of their trousers, by which we finally toppled them over the rail like two bags of barley.

They then picked themselves up and we handed them back the rifles. Trying to assume some air of dignity, one of them said:

'We demand to see your papers.'

We led them down below and they seemed glad to sit in front of the fire. The mate, a kind-hearted soul, took pity on their condition and gave them each a cup of tea.

I thought that a fitting end to this comedy, which might easily have been a tragedy, would be to deny them that which they sought to inquire into. I felt sure that they did not know a ship's papers from a mission hymn sheet. So while they drank their tea I rummaged in my drawer and pulled out the ship's assignment (a document concerning the plan and construction of the vessel), an out-of-date transire and an old Bill of Lading, all of which happened to be tied together with a piece of silk which made them look like valuable papers.

These I handed to the leader of the two-man armed party. He unfolded the assignment, glanced at it with a show of authority, off-handedly turned over the old transire and Bill of Lading and seemed satisfied. He handed them back to me, not knowing that the ship's papers (her register, licence, customs clearance, Admiralty orders and route instructions) lay in the locker behind him.

'Your papers seem quite in order, captain,' he remarked briefly. 'I'm sorry we have had to trouble you, but when you did not answer our hail the skipper became suspicious. Routine, y' know, what!'

And off they went, leaving Jerry and me to our peaceful cabin comforts and to reflect on what silly asses the war had brought upon the water.

MAN OVERBOARD IN THE MIDDLE OF THE PACIFIC

Sailing without lifejackets, life-rafts and emergency beacons was commonplace 40 years ago; when you went overboard you did not expect to live. Ben Pester did go over the side but survived to tell the tale

Eight years after World War II, a young Royal Navy engineering officer Ben Pester was to be given a new role on a ship in his native New Zealand. He decided to sail there rather than take more conventional transport and the Ministry of Defence agreed it would add to his experience and he was granted leave to do it. His boat for the 14 000 mile voyage from Plymouth to Auckland was a 39 ft gaff yawl, *Tern II*, once owned by legendary yachtsman Claud Worth.

He interviewed many young men to join him and decided on Peter Fox a yachtsman from Portsmouth and in 1953 they set off.

Tern II had no radio, GPS, electronics or even cabin lights. She carried no lifejackets and no life-raft; they navigated with sextant and used oil lamps for illumination.

Ironically it was the traditional method of recording miles sailed—the Walker Patent Log—which was to prove a better life-saver than more modern safety kit.

Having successfully crossed the Atlantic, cruised through the Caribbean and transited the Panama Canal the pair were halfway to the Marquesas from the Galapagos when one morning disaster struck. Peter was fast asleep below, it being Ben's watch. In order to answer the call of nature, Ben lashed the helm and got the *Tern II* sailing herself: not a difficult task with a long, deep-keeled boat. He then walked along the leeward deck and using both hands to adjust his dress while leaning on the after shroud, *Tern II* suddenly lurched from an unexpected wave and pitched Ben head first into the sea.

Tern II was cracking along in the trade winds under her downwind rig making six miles nearer to the Marquesas every hour and Ben desperately clawing at her rail was soon left astern watching his sweet-lined ship sailing away from him. His shouts failed to raise Peter, but it was then he remembered the spinning log line trailing behind *Tern II's* stern and clocking those six miles each hour. The line is turned by a 'fish', a metal rotator with fins. Ben swam across to the quickly disappearing line and got his hands round it. He had the presence of mind to let the line slip through his hands slowly as he put his grip on it for fear that a sudden grasp, adding 13 stone deadweight to the thin plaited line would snap it.

With his heart pounding at the thought of the screws holding the dial mounted on the gunnel being pulled out, he closed his hands over the line. It held. But now Ben's head was continually dragged beneath the waves and he had to struggle to keep his mouth above water. The line was also cutting into his hands.

How long could this go on?

Fortunately the faithful *Tern II* started to luff up into the wind: partly it was the untended helm, partly Ben's weight shifting her course. Then something in Peter's sub-conscious made him wake up. He later said he couldn't explain it. But the senses of all sailors after a long time at sea become acute. The slightest alteration of the ship's order will bring a man from the deepest of slumbers.

Peter unlashed the helm, luffed *Tern II* round into the wind and started hauling Ben in.

He then lowered a bight of rope to act as a step and Ben clambered aboard. Neither of them said anything, but both had a tot of rum and got the boat sailing towards the Marquesas once more.

PILOT ERROR CAUSES SHIPWRECK AND DEATH

The Thames Estuary's sandbanks have claimed many ships over the years. But the wreck of the *Indian Chief* is still talked about in lifeboat circles

The full rigged ship *Indian Chief*, of Liverpool, left Middlesborough on 2 January 1881 with general cargo for Yokohama. Her captain and 27 crew were in the hands of a pilot whose job it was to secure her safe passage down the North Sea, through the Dover Strait and as far down Channel as Beachy Head.

On the morning of the 4th the ship passed Lowestoft, about seven miles on her starboard beam. But now, as the land and the ship's course diverged it would be the dreaded sands of the Thames Estuary which would be under her lee. A bitterly cold north-east wind was pushing the *Indian Chief* along at five knots under full sail, including topgallant sails and royals. That night, at around 20.00, the wind began to freshen, and the royals, flying jib, and mainsail were taken in. Just before midnight they sighted Orfordness, Suffolk, about seven miles away. The ship was steering west of south when it would have been a better course to have been sailing east of south: as the powerful flood tide was setting them westwards towards the long fingers of hard sand which muzzle the Thames Estuary's entrance.

The pilot's error had the ship sailing between two of the estuary's most dangerous banks, and what's more it was at night: the Knock and the Long Sand. They were enjoying a fair wind from the north-east, and a course could easily have been laid to take her outside the Long Sand and clear of all hazards.

When he realised his error the pilot panicked and tried to tack the ship back, through the Knock Deep, against wind and tide. Yet having entered this channel there was no reason he could not have continued through it and cleared the sands at the southern end.

The ship fell into irons on one tack as she neared the Long Sand and as the breakers could be heard and seen glowing under the stars, the *Indian Chief's* crew tried wearing ship: bringing her round stern first to the wind, but unfortunately in their haste to get her clear the spanker-boom sheet fouled the wheel and, out of control, she struck the eastern side of the sands broadside to.

As it was nearly high water she was well on top as the starboard anchor was dropped, and 50 fathoms of chain were paid out to try to bring the vessel's head to the wind, to stop her driving further on. Her sails were kept standing to try and steady her, but as soon as the tide had fallen, they were clewed up. Rockets were then sent up and a flare burnt. By now a furious gale had sprung up from the north-east and in the words of the first mate William Lloyd: 'She was a soft-wood built ship and she trembled as though she would go to pieces like a pack of cards. Sheets and halliards were let go, but no man dared go aloft as every moment threatened to bring the spars crashing about us, and the thundering and beating of the canvas made the masts buckle and jump like fishing-rods'.

Eventually their flares were answered by flares from two lightships the *Sunk* and the *Knock*, but during the following day as no assistance had arrived, the shipwrecked sailors tried to launch the ship's boats, but they capsized and two men were drowned. Then the *Indian Chief* broke her back and as the second night came on all hands took to the rigging: the master, the first mate, and 16 hands going into the mizzen rigging, whilst the pilot and eight hands got into the fore rigging. During the night the first mate left the mizzen and joined those in the fore rigging, which he thought had a better chance of standing. About two hours before daylight the mainmast went over the side, carrying with it the mizzenmast, and all the crew on it were drowned.

All this time lifeboats from Aldeburgh, Clacton and Harwich had tried but failed to get to the wreck. The Ramsgate lifeboat, *Bradford* had better luck. Though furthest away, with assistance from the paddle-tug *Vulcan*, she had been towed to the scene. In the words of her coxswain, Charles Fish: 'The *Vulcan*, when she met the first of the seas, was thrown up like a ball, and you could see her starboard paddle revolving in the air, high enough for a coach to pass under and when she struck the hollow she dished a sea over her bows that left only her stern showing'.

The hardy Ramsgate men, sustained with several tots of rum, had spent the whole night shivering in the lifeboat, waiting for daylight to effect a rescue. The following morning they set sail, dropped the tug towline, and succeeded in taking the remaining 12 crew off the wreck.

On the wrecked mizzenmast the captain squatted with his arms folded, seemingly watching the rescue taking place. When Coxswain Fish ordered his men to pull for the wreckage to take him off, the *Indian Chief's* crew told him: 'He's been dead four hours'. So the lifeboatmen left the half-frozen, eerily staring corpse behind and returned to Ramsgate where all 12 were landed except the second mate, brother of the ship's master, who died on the way from exposure.

A newspaper reporter from the *Daily Telegraph* described the survivors coming ashore: 'One by one they came along the pier, the most dismal procession it was ever my lot to behold – 11 live but scarcely living men ... there was blood on the faces of some circled with a white encrustation of salt which also filled the hollows of their eyes and streaked their hair like snow. Shivering, rolling their eyes, clenching their teeth, their chilled fingers pressed into the palms of their hands they passed out of sight'.

A subsequent hearing concluded: 'The cause of the casualty was no doubt the mistake of the pilot in shaping a course without making any allowance for the set of the flood tide to the westward. This brought him between the Knock and Long Sands, and when in that position, instead of running down through the Knock Deep, or if necessary coming to an anchor, he chooses to tack over towards the Long Sand until he strikes upon it'.

FAMILY DAY-TRIP BECOMES RESCUE AT SEA

Mike Peyton is the world's greatest yachting cartoonist – but there were no smiles to be seen when he nearly lost his family and boat in the North Sea

Yachting cartoonist Mike Peyton has spent a lifetime depicting the calamities of those who go down to the sea in sailing boats. Sometimes his subjects have recognised themselves in the published results of his observations: with varying reactions.

What is not so well known is that while Mike might seem a callous observer to those who have become his victims, he is equally merciless on himself and some of his best work has come from his own cock-ups.

Of these, the most dangerous occasion was when he went for a day sail with his wife Kath and their two baby daughters, Hilary and Veronica.

Sugar Creek was a 30 ft gaff cutter built of pitch pine some three decades earlier and Mike had put guard rails on her, laced up with chicken wire to stop the children pitching over the side. They had left their mooring in Clements Green Creek on the River Crouch, Essex and because of engine problems abandoned their plan to visit Whitstable to see some old friends, en route to the West Country, and instead sailed up the River Roach to Paglesham for the night. Overnight the wind increased to gale force and they were windbound off the tiny Essex hamlet for five days.

With their holiday time ebbing away any thoughts of setting off down Channel were abandoned and Mike was just keen to get some sailing in anywhere as soon as the wind eased up.

With a morning forecast of south-westerly Force 4 to 5 backing southerly later and freshening to Force 6 they set off hoping to get in somewhere before the wind increased again.

But bashing against the south-west wind, with the tide kicking up large seas, soon found the boat's weakness. Her shrouds suddenly went slack and Mike and Kath fought to get her sails down before they lost the mast over the side. Kath ran *Sugar Creek* off before the wind while Mike went below to investigate. He discovered the mast had not been set down on the keel properly: it had been out of its step. As it worked back and forth as they tacked to windward it had suddenly dropped into the slot with the consequent loosening of the rigging.

Under staysail alone the boat wallowed along while Mike worked out a plan of action, but then they saw a big ballooning star in the sky followed by a muffled report. It was from the Barrow lightship: a warning flare telling the sailors they were heading for the East Barrow Sand. Then they hit it. Fortunately the tide was rising and with the staysail backed they got the boat round and heading back for deep water while Mike tightened up the rigging as best he could and re-set the gaff mainsail.

It was not set for long before the increasing wind tore it from the gaff: all the luff slides had slipped out of the track and it flogged for a while before becoming a write off.

Now all they could do was run before the wind under staysail alone for Harwich.

The sky got darker and the wind blew harder, but their morale was raised when they picked up one of the Barrow buoys marking the Barrow Deep and realised the tide had now turned and together with the wind was sending *Sugar Creek* rapidly north towards shelter.

At dusk they picked up one of the Gunfleet Channel buoys and on top of the waves they could see the lights of Harwich. Rain set in and Kath went below to make soup for the two girls who were scared but quiet. Kath was sick from the Primus stove fumes but stoically served the soup.

Mike was by now aware that the beamy old double-ender would not fetch Harwich just under headsail alone with a beam wind and tide. He was also aware that as they ran on past Harwich he was out of charts.

'Never mind she's riding like an old duck,' he said delightedly.

Kath was unimpressed: 'Yes, but the children. If we miss Harwich where are we going to land up?'

'Norway at this rate,' said Mike, enjoying the sail.

They were by now well past Harwich and nearing the Cutler shoal off Bawdsey in Suffolk.

Kath wanted to signal a pilot boat on her way into Harwich. Mike wouldn't hear of it and considered anchoring.

'In this ? Out here?' remonstrated Kath.

Then Veronica was sick.

It was by now 20.00 and they'd been under way 16 hours and not got very far.

Mike relented and Kath, who had learned Morse Code in the Girl Guides, used a hand torch to signal SOS at a passing ship.

It was the British Rail ferry ship *Suffolk* on her way to Harwich from Holland and they ranged alongside and in the rolling sea smashed against the yacht's mast, slackening off the rigging but this time more decisively. Then on the next wave the great steel and rubber fending strake of the ferry crushed and splintered the top of *Sugar Creek's* decks. Mike watched hopelessly as his boat was beaten up, meanwhile Kath handed the children one at a time on the top of the wave into the arms 'of a man in a string vest' standing in a lit doorway.

Kath and then Mike joined them.

'The children were being carried away by two burly sailors along what appeared to be a railway siding,' said Kath, 'Stumbling over railway lines I ran after them like a ewe deprived of its lambs'.

Hilary thought it was great: 'We've been shipwrecked like Rupert Bear,' she said.

Sugar Creek was taken under tow but a plank had sprung, she was taking on water and the tow soon parted and she was left in the black North Sea and reported as a danger to shipping.

In Harwich they were given a room at the Pier Hotel.

'We seemed to have failed so abysmally that it did not seem there was any more to say,' recalled Kath, 'Everybody being so kind made it worse'.

Next day *Sugar Creek* was towed into Harwich by a Trinity House vessel. She was half full of water and required a major re-build.

Both crew and ship had survived, but not without lessons learned.

'It was not the boat that had failed us,' Kath said, 'it was ourselves who had not been equal to the occasion'.

And Mike still has the original cartoon of the rescue to prove it.

THE CURSE OF ILL-GOTTEN GAINS

This young merchant sailor and his shipmate were rescued at sea by pirates. One of them became a pirate himself, the other resisted. Which was the wisest choice?

The fast flowing tides of the River Humber which drains Yorkshire and North Lincolnshire, run so hard that buoys marking the fairway are shaped like ships to withstand the pressure on their moorings. Many lads who grow up along this boiling, almost orange-coloured river become some of the best sailors in the world. A local saying among the tough fishermen along those shores was: 'We're used to drowning', when the Board of Trade offered safety equipment to the sailing trawler crews.

Things were little different in the early 15th century when William Cummins of Hull was apprenticed to a master mariner from that port, Thomas Kingsley owner of the coasting brig *Speedy*.

In a heavy north-west gale off the island of Heligoland in the German Bight the *Speedy* foundered with the loss of all hands except Cummins and an old seadog called Michael Shepherd who both clung on to a drifting spar until they were picked up by a North Sea pirate Captain Jinks master of the *Tyger*.

But the *Tyger* did not stop to drop the men back in Yorkshire. Instead she sped on down the English Channel pursued by two of King Edward IV's warships *Swallow* and *Garland* whose instructions were to bring Jinks ashore for trial and certain death in the chains at Wapping Stairs on the River Thames where many a pirate had three tides wash over his corpse: part civic revenge and part deterrent.

The ships caught up with the *Tyger* off Land's End and at night the pirate's crew drank all the hooch aboard then disembarked in longboats. But the inebriated sailors were lost as their boats sank in a vicious cross sea knocked up by wind against tide.

The only boat still afloat was Captain Jinks' who had a chest of treasure and both Cummins and Shepherd with him. He told the men to pull away as fast as they could for he had lit a trail of gunpowder to despatch the *Tyger*. When she exploded the night seas were lit up, momentarily, for miles around and a falling spar killed Jinks. The two shipwrecked men, now shipwrecked once more, escaped unseen by the warships and at dawn they committed Jinks' corpse to the deep with Cummins muttering a Latin prayer for his soul.

The two men eventually struggled ashore in Penzance and made their way home to Hull. The story of their lucky survival from the shipwreck of the *Speedy* made no mention of their rescue by a North Sea pirate, nor of their windfall.

Funded by the treasure Cummins and Shepherd set off in another brig, the *Rainbow*, with a crew of 23 men in a search of fortune on African shores. They made landfall at Cape Palmas in what is now Liberia but by then most of Cummins' crew – apart from Shepherd and five others – had mutinied. An attempt by one sailor to murder his captain with an axe was foiled and the would-be assailant was hanged on the yard arm. This did nothing to quell the unrest among the other mutineers and while Cummins and Shepherd were ashore in a tent trading beads, knives and other glittering trinkets for ivory and gold dust, the mutineers burst in with a second attempt on Cummins' life and that of his loyal crew.

Two Africans were stabbed in the affray, which Cummins and Shepherd survived, after shooting two mutineers dead and chasing the others into the forest.

They immediately returned to the ship and overwhelmed the remaining mutineers before shackling them below. One of the captives was fatally injured however, and determined not to die alone set fire to a barrel of tar.

By the time Cummins discovered the fire it was too late to save the ship so he cut her cable allowing her to drift ashore where he at least hoped to save his valuable cargo of ivory and gold. He and his faithful crew meanwhile rowed ashore in a longboat.

Their negotiations with the locals had been well conducted and the Africans fed and clothed them and helped chase down and kill off the remaining mutineers who had fled to the forest. The longboat was only big enough to carry half the crew back to Europe, along the coast. So it was decided by lot that Shepherd, two men and three boys would make the long and perilous voyage with the gold remaining from the wreck of the *Rainbow*, purchase another ship and return to rescue Cummins and the remaining men.

But the years and months of piracy had turned Shepherd's head and when he eventually arrived back in Hull he announced Cummins was dead, hoping to use the gold dust to fund his own voyage of fortune.

But Cummins, too, had learnt the low cunning of his pirate masters and as a safeguard against Shepherd's possible treachery had given a letter to one of Shepherd's lads, John Darling, to be handed to Cummins' wife back in Hull.

As Shepherd prepared his own vessel of fortune, the *Mary Rose*, he ran out of money. He was visited by a slim young man who offered to underwrite the balance as long as he could have a berth aboard. Shepherd readily agreed and in June 1476 the *Mary Rose* sailed back to West Africa on the second voyage of fortune hunting.

The slim young man turned out to be Cummins' wife in disguise who was successfully reunited with her husband at the voyage end.

Meanwhile Shepherd, who had turned completely piratical, and many of his men were massacred by Africans as they started raping local women – and stealing ivory and gold rather than trading as Cummins had done.

Cummins eventually returned to Hull and carried on his trading, this time with the Levant. He died a rich man beside the fast-flowing River Humber.

SAILING TO THE WRONG HEMISPHERE

Solo sailor and three-times circumnavigator Leslie Powles recalls his first single-handed adventure setting sail for Barbados, but arriving in Brazil

Back in the 1970s I chanced on an advertisement in a yachting magazine, 'Come to Liverpool and build your own Nor-West 34, hull and deck, £1 300'. I promptly made an appointment and then spent two years building *Solitaire*, with help and advice from two friends.

She was baptised in the spring of 1975 at Lymington. The launch went without a hitch. Everyone was impressed with my plans to sail around the world single-handed.

My first sailing lesson took place a few weeks later and then I took *Solitaire* out alone, for the first time. I decided a cautious approach would be best, with the engine on slow tick-over. If I bumped into other boats only small pieces would be removed. The mechanics of sailing were never to trouble me, but I deeply regretted not having had the opportunity to learn in dinghies as a boy. Bad habits take years to break, whether swinging a golf club, driving a car or sailing a yacht.

At 0900 Monday morning 18 August 1975 I had accumulated eight hours sailing time on *Solitaire*, two of them solo. Compared with this vast amount of knowledge, my navigation was a little weak.

My next port of call was Barbados in the West Indies. The plan was to sail down the English Channel, turn sharp left 300 miles into the Atlantic, then sail between the Azores and Portugal and fork right onto latitude 13° 20′ until the island appeared over the horizon.

My navigational equipment consisted of plastic sextant, Walker trailing log, Seafarer depth sounder, RDF set, portable radio, old car clock, almanac and Bible. A major mistake was not to carry the Admiralty Book of Radio Signals, listing stations around the world.

The wind blew free but the rent man called that evening, first with a light tapping on the door, followed by a more insistent banging and whistling. As the wind increased, the sea became choppy and I reduced the headsail to working jib. Darkness descended and Portland Bill lighthouse started flashing. I came about and headed south. France was 60 miles away. Then a fog descended, thick, grey banks which prompted me to start the engine to maintain a compass course. The outlines of large ships waltzed by, partnering *Solitaire* in a dance of disaster. The trailing log line got tangled around the skeg, so I had no idea how far *Solitaire* travelled. Tuesday morning saw us completely lost. My RDF set could have supplied the answers but the batteries were flat.

When the fog lifted, we were in the western end of a vast bay. I motored over to a young lady in a dinghy and shouted, 'Ahoy there, missy, could you please tell me where you anchor in Falmouth Harbour?'

'About 100 miles westwards!' came a shrieked reply. Brixham was where I made my first attempt at anchoring. Later, having made landfall in Falmouth, I bought a roasted chicken, some vegetables, and prepared for my first long voyage across the Atlantic.

If I could make 100 miles a day I would be content and, should I fail to achieve this distance, who cared? I didn't have to be in a certain place at a given time. The crazy world could wait until I chose to join it again. When I found *Solitaire* slamming into heavy seas, I would drop all sail, batten myself below and read or sleep. If the winds turned into storms and they were aft of the mast I would simply run with them on a broad reach under working jib. My boat was strong, so I was never frightened.

When the RDF signals faded, 300 miles into the Atlantic, I had to depend on dead reckoning and the sextant. After ten days at sea I read the instructions in Reed's Almanac and used my plastic sextant to take my first sight for latitude. My old car clock lost 40 seconds or so a day, which meant I had to guess when the sun would reach its maximum height.

Solitaire picked up the trade winds, constant at Force 3 to 4 over our stern. I started to learn the importance of a varied food supply. Nearly all the food on board was tinned: the fresh food had been eaten in the first week.

The main event of our Atlantic crossing took place on 23 September 1975, at precisely 1400 hours GMT. It would be many weeks before I learned the importance of this day and the changes it would make to my life. All that is recorded in the ship's log for that day is 'Distance travelled 2 442 miles. Latitude 23° 41′ North'. From now on things would happen that made no sense. Was I under the influence of the Bermuda Triangle, where ships and aircraft had vanished? Day after day we pushed further south into dangers that subsequently would make me shudder at my stupidity.

One day we were beating into a breaking sea with a long swell, *Solitaire* buried her nose, waves streaming up her decks towards the cockpit. I needed to drop the large genoa. I grabbed the forestay in panic, drawing in breath as though it were my last, before sinking into a green world, which sucked me away from *Solitaire*. Water filled my nose and I choked. After what seemed a lifetime I was lifted clear, terrified, trying to draw breath into burning lungs, spitting out mouthfuls of sea.

At that moment, strangely, I stopped being afraid. My fear was replaced by anger and I screamed obscenities, using every backstreet gutter word I could remember, even managing to invent a few. Within minutes using hand-like steel claws, I had changed sails and was back in the cockpit, sucking the salt from my lips which I spat over the side. It was not until I had towelled myself down, and was sitting with a cup of tea, that my hands stopped shaking. Then I began to think about the strange Jekyll and Hyde character I had met on the foredeck. If I could control him and harness his anger to give me the strength to survive, I would learn a valuable lesson.

At 2200 on 13 October, after being at sea for 57 days and having logged 4 340 miles, a lighthouse flashed, which should not have been there. By dead reckoning, we were still 200 miles from Barbados. Our noon sight that day put us more than 80 miles above the island. My sole chart, which covered the whole Caribbean, reduced Barbados to one inch and showed two lighthouses but no flashing codes. I headed out to sea to await morning.

Dawn found *Solitaire* sailing on a southerly course parallel to an island with sandy beaches, palm trees and hills in the distance. A few dhow-type vessels about 40ft long with large triangular sails were in sight, with three dark-skinned natives on board.

Solitaire was facing huge breaking seas. I was halfway to the tiller when the air filled with flying spray. She was lifted sideways and struck viciously by a gigantic hammer, which stopped her dead. The boat fell on her side, lockers burst open in the cabin and I was bombarded by books, tins and bottles. The seas had her, like a tiger bringing down a fawn, swinging her in a complete circle. I tried to escape through the hatch but solid water flung me back, the cabin darkened by green shades that covered its windows.

Later, I emerged shamefaced, embarrassed by the dangers I had left *Solitaire* to face alone and hoping that some small part of her would be found so that my family would not spend years wondering if I were alive or dead. The mast still stood, but my home was wrecked.

Solitaire was held in soft sand. The reef she had survived lay to one side. I started pumping but it took an age to clear the water in the cabin. *Solitaire* started to come alive again. I thought of using the engine. I turned the key and it roared into life and *Solitaire* shuddered with pleasure. As I pulled in her sails, she leaned, sighed and moved. Life was full again. We were off to Barbados.

We were still in sandy seas that stretched to the horizon. At noon, a second island appeared on the hazy horizon. Was it St. Lucia? A few hours later I realised the two islands were merging and we were entering the mouth of a river. There was nothing in the Caribbean that looked like this!

A Spanish-style village began to appear above a bay to starboard, first a church, then white buildings with red-tiled roofs. I carried on up the river which, just before dark, ended in forest, and dropped anchor. The sky was full of stinging insects which feasted heartily off me through the night. By dawn, my face was puffed and swollen.

A few days later, after leaving the river, I anchored in a large bay with fishing boats. I awoke to find *Solitaire* lying on her side. At least I could examine the wounds from her encounter with the reef. An area of hull had been pushed in the depth of a dinner plate. There were scratches and gouges, but her GRP skin was a solid inch thick.

By now a crowd of natives gathered. I decided to inspect my stock of 18 bottles of spirits and some 600 English cigarettes which, as I was a non-smoker, were mostly for trade. I came across about 40 sodden yachting magazines and took them on deck, intending to dump them. A girl reached up, so I gave her one. Next minute I was besieged by fighting, screaming women. I dished out half a dozen bottles of whisky and gin to the men and started handing out cigarettes. While this was going on, I tried to hold some kind of a conversation without much luck. Suddenly, I heard the name 'Pele'.

'Football!' I shouted, and pretended to dribble a ball. Pointing to myself I said, 'Golf!' I still had a set of golf clubs on board so fetched them, made a round hole in the sand, marched back 150 yards, selected my trusty five iron and asked the admiring public to stand back. On my fourth attempt I managed to move a ball ten feet.

Around noon a Land Rover came down the beach with two uniformed men and a civilian. My passport and ship's papers were handed over and for the first time I heard the name Tutoia, the fishing village two miles or so away at the other end of the bay.

When the tide came and *Solitaire* floated, I was piloted through a winding channel until I had my first sight of Tutoia, a dirty beach with a single wooden jetty and a few red-roofed bungalows among scattered palm trees.

I found a stainless-steel mirror, which I cleaned and polished. The reflection surely was not me. Not this ugly mass of blisters and yellow, weeping sores? The ginger beard was encrusted with filth, the eyes barely visible, just red swollen lids with slits which started to run as I became sorry – not for myself, but for the poor fool in the mirror.

I was told a naval officer wanted to see me and tried to make myself presentable.

In pigeon English Lieutenant Orland Sapana asked: 'English?'

'Si, yes, English'. I replied.

He said he was Brazilian, which confused me.

'St. Lucia? Brazilian?' I queried, shaking my head.

'Si, si'. He stretched his arms wide and said, 'Brazil'.

For a moment I stared at the charts, expecting my head to explode. I was in Brazil, 1 000 miles south of the Caribbean island of St. Lucia! How could I have made such an incredible blunder?

That afternoon a local deputation from the village urged me to go to hospital. There would be no charge they said, apart from medicines and food.

On my return to *Solitaire*, I re-read the instructions for taking a noon sight for latitude. On 23 September, when halfway across the Atlantic, the declination had changed from North to South (the sun moving south of the equator) but I had continued to add the figure instead of subtract. I believed my latitude to be 14° 40′N but I had hit the Brazilian coast about 1° 20′ south of the equator! Sao Luis is the capital and port in that area of Brazil, its call sign SLI. Had I carried the Admiralty List of Radio Signals I would have found that St. Lucia's call sign in the Windward Islands was, in fact, SLU!

* * *

This is an edited extract from *Hands Open*, by Leslie Powles, Kenneth Mason Publications, 1987.

HANGING BY A THREAD FROM A SHIPWRECK

George Millar was a yachtsman and a true hero whose life was more of a ripping yarn than any work of fiction

Appointed the *Daily Express*'s correspondent in Paris, in 1939, George Millar stayed only long enough to hear Britain declaring war on Germany before returning home to join up. As a soldier in World War II, he was wounded and taken prisoner in the Western Desert. He later escaped and made his way from Munich home to Britain, via France and Spain. Then he joined the Special Operations Executive and was parachuted back behind enemy lines in France where he helped organise resistance groups. His newspaperman's quick thinking was put to the test when he was with the Maquis. Challenged by an enemy sentry he shot the man dead with a pistol fired through his overcoat pocket. He was decorated with the DSO, the Military Cross, the Legion d'Honneur and the Croix de Guerre.

But, exhausted after such a dangerous war he set off for some serious cruising with his half-Spanish wife Isabel, first of all through the French canals to Greece aboard their first yacht *Truant* and later to the Mediterranean again, this time round the outside aboard their 40 ft yacht *Serica*, a 16-ton Bermudan sloop designed by Robert Clark.

In 1950 they sailed from Lymington down along the north Brittany coast, across Biscay and down the Portuguese coast until Millar contracted food poisoning from a full plate of shellfish during a run ashore.

His wife was already handicapped by a broken left arm from a horse-riding accident during a fox hunt back at their home in Dorset. The arm was still knitting back together in plaster cast and she could not manage the boat alone.

As Millar felt sick and weary from his illness he broke out into a sweat one night watch and fought to stay at the helm until daybreak. His strength ebbing away rapidly, he left Isabel at the helm while he went below, changed his clothes rubbed himself all over, took a stiff draught of brandy and returned on deck. But it was no good he was on the point of collapse and so the decision was made to con the boat into an anchorage – far from ideal – in Sines Bay. The anchor chain jumped off the windlass in the heavy sea and Millar made a grab for it tearing the skin off his fingers and ripping a fingernail off.

They watched to make sure the heavy boat was not dragging. They laid out two anchors to make sure and Millar bent on a spring from the yacht's mast to both anchor cables to prevent them snubbing. Then he collapsed below to try and sleep off his sickness in the soaking wet saloon: it had been a rough passage. Isabel was seasick from the pitching motion of the boat which was virtually anchored in the open sea.

By evening the weather had eased and they managed to launch the yacht's dinghy and rowed ashore to be greeted by scores of curious fishermen.

For four nights Millar writhed in sweat in the room of a hotel. Isabel had paid a couple of fishermen to keep an eye on *Serica*, but was disheartened when she looked out one morning to see that all the yacht's lights had been left on unnecessarily draining the batteries.

When Millar regained his health and the pair got back aboard they discovered that *Serica's* guardians had got through 10 litres of wine, a bottle of Madeira, all their cigarettes – kept aboard as bargaining chips – three pounds of cheese, all the ship's bread and all the tinned food.

Millar was furious and of the fisherman they had entrusted to organise a watch system, Millar wrote: 'I had thought of freeing one of the cockpit winch-handles, eighteen inches of steel, nicely balanced and terminating in a round steel ball with which to say hullo'.

But a bigger shock was to come.

Millar discovered that the spring to stop the anchors snubbing had been unbent and as a result the warp to the secondary anchor had chafed through and was lost. This in turn meant the boat then swung just to the chain of the bower anchor which had run right out.

Below, a puzzled Millar noticed that there was no chain hanging down from the hawse pipe into the chain locker. To his horror he found that the bitter end – shackled to a screw eye in the keel – had torn the screw-eye from its fastenings and snatched it up to the hawse hole which led on deck. Only the fact that the fixing had stopped lengthwise under the edge of the hawse hole had prevented the chain running away completely and *Serica* drifting onto the rocks just a few hundred yards astern.

PART FIVE

Adventure

A REAL LIFE MONSTER OF THE DEEP

Giant creatures of the ocean depths have long been the off-watch nightmares of sailors. One night crewman Frank Bullen watched a moonlit battle between two leviathans of the deep

While voyaging on the whaling ship *Cachalot*, the London crewman, Frank Bullen, was very peeved when he was obliged to stand an extra watch. But it gave him the chance to witness a surreal battle between two giant creatures of the deep whose deadly embrace had forced them to the surface. The story is best told by Frank himself:

> The third mate being ill I had been invested with the questionable honour of standing his watch, on account of my sea experience and growing favour with the chief. Very bitterly did I resent the privilege I remember, being so tired and sleepy that I knew not how to keep awake. I did not imagine that anything

would happen to make me prize that night's experience for the rest of my life, or I should have taken matters with a far better grace.

At about eleven p.m. I was leaning over the lee rail, gazing steadily at the bright surface of the sea, where the intense radiance of the tropical moon made a broad path like a pavement of burnished silver. Eyes that saw not, mind only confusedly conscious of my surroundings, were mine; but suddenly I started to my feet with an exclamation, and stared with all my might at the strangest sight I ever saw. There was a violent commotion in the sea right where the moon's rays were concentrated, so great that, remembering our position, I was at first inclined to alarm all hands; for I had often heard of volcanic islands suddenly lifting their heads from the depths below, or disappearing in a moment, and, with Sumatra's chain of active volcanoes so near, I felt doubtful indeed of what was now happening. Getting the night-glasses out of the cabin scuttle, where they were always hung in readiness, I focussed them on the troubled spot, perfectly satisfied by a short examination that neither volcano nor earthquake had anything to do with what was going on; yet so vast were the forces engaged that I might well have been excused for my first supposition. A very large sperm whale was locked in deadly conflict with a cuttle-fish, or squid, almost as large as himself, whose interminable tentacles seemed to enlace the whole of his great body. The head of the whale especially seemed a perfect net-work of writhing arms – naturally, I suppose, for it appeared as if the whale had the tail part of the mollusc in his jaws, and, in a business-like, methodical way, was sawing through it. By the side of the black columnar head of the whale appeared the head of the great squid, as awful an object as one could well imagine even in a fevered dream. Judging as carefully as possible, I estimated it to be at least as large as one of our pipes, which contained three hundred and fifty gallons; but it may have been, and probably was, a good deal larger. The eyes were very remarkable from their size and blackness, which, contrasted with the livid whiteness of the head, made their appearance all the more striking. They were, at least, a foot in diameter, and, seen under such conditions, looked decidedly eerie and hobgoblin-like. All around the combatants were numerous sharks, like jackals round a lion, ready to share the feast, and apparently assisting in the destruction of the huge cephalopod. So the titanic struggle went on, in perfect silence as far as we were concerned, because, even had there been any noise, our distance from the scene of conflict would not have permitted us to hear it.

Thinking that such a sight ought not to be missed by the captain, I overcame my dread of him sufficiently to call him, and tell him of what was taking place. He met my remarks with such a furious burst of anger at my daring to disturb him for such a cause, that I fled precipitately on deck again, having the remainder of the vision to myself, for none of the others cared sufficiently for such things to lose five minutes' sleep in witnessing them. The conflict ceased, the sea resumed its placid calm, and nothing remained to tell of the fight but a strong odour of fish, as of a bank of seaweed left by the tide in the blazing sun. Eight bells struck, and 1 went below to a troubled sleep, wherein all the awful monsters that an over-excited brain could conjure up pursued me through the gloomy caves of ocean, or mocked my pigmy efforts to escape. The occasions upon which these gigantic cuttle-fish appear at the sea surface must, I think, be very rare. From their construction, they appear fitted only to grope among the rocks at the bottom of the ocean. Their mode of progression is backward, by the forcible ejection of a jet of water from an orifice in the neck, beside the rectum or cloaca. Consequently their normal position is head downward, and with tentacles spread out like the ribs of an umbrella–eight of them at least; the two long ones, like the antenna of an insect, rove unceasingly around, seeking prey. The imagination can hardly picture a more terrible object than one of these huge monsters brooding in the ocean depths, the gloom of his surroundings increased by the inky fluid (sepia) which he secretes in copious quantities, every cup-shaped disc, of the hundreds with which the restless tentacles are furnished, ready at the slightest touch to grip whatever is near, not only by suction, but by the great claws set all round within its circle. And in the centre of this net-work of living traps is the chasm-like mouth, with its enormous parrot-beak, ready to rend piecemeal whatever is held by the tentacles. The very thought of it makes one's flesh crawl. Well did Michelet term them "the insatiable nightmares of the sea." Yet, but for them, how would such great creatures as the sperm whale be fed? Unable, from their bulk, to capture small fish except by accident, and, by the absence of a sieve of baleen, precluded from subsisting upon tiny crustacea, the cachalots seem to be confined for their diet to cuttle-fish, and, from their point of view, the bigger the latter are the better. How big they may become in the depths of the sea, no man knoweth; but it is unlikely that even the vast specimens seen are full-sized, since they have only come to the surface under abnormal conditions, like the one I have attempted to describe, who had evidently, been dragged up by his relentless foe.

TREASURE ISLAND

Thirteen men spent three months on a deserted volcanic islet digging for the lost treasure of Lima. They encountered landslides, ocean swells, but most horrible of all . . . invasion by land crabs

A 64-foot gaff cutter is a big boat to handle, but even so, it does not require a crew of 12. Yet that was the number of English 'gentleman adventurers' who, under the command of their skipper Edward Frederick Knight, 37, arrived aboard the *Alerte* off the forbidding coast of Trinidad (not to be confused with the much larger Caribbean island of the same name), near Brazil in 1889. They were there to make their fortune and although the sailing of the cutter from England had been a steep learning curve for many of them, their real test was about to begin: digging and mining the volcanic rock of Trinidad for the lost treasure of Lima.

E. F. Knight, as he signed himself, was no ordinary gold digger. He was a successful barrister, former soldier and correspondent for *The*

Times. He had checked out as far as he could the story told to him by an old sea captain from South Shields who had himself tried to excavate the fortune believed to be buried on Trinidad. This sea captain had in turn been told by a terminally ill pirate, a Russian Finn who was part of the original burial party, that the treasure was stashed under a mountain on the island called the Sugar Loaf.

The treasure was believed to have been part of the £6 million worth of bullion, plate, jewels and coined gold which had been en route back to Spain from Lima after South America's Spanish rule came to an abrupt end in 1819. Many ships were carrying the booty and several were attacked by contemporary pirates. As well as Trinidad some of the hoard was supposed to be buried on Cocos Island, in the Pacific, part of what is today, Costa Rica.

But it was the Atlantic island of Trinidad that the armed crew of the *Alerte* spotted in late November after a three-month cruise from Southampton with stops en route. Knight described it thus:

> The north side is the most barren and desolate portion of the island, and appears to be utterly inaccessible. Here the mountains rise sheer from the boiling surf – fantastically shaped of volcanic rock; cloven by frightful ravines; lowering in perpendicular precipices; in places overhanging threateningly, and, where the mountains have been shaken to pieces by the fires and earthquakes of volcanic action, huge landslips slope steeply into the yawning ravines – landslips of black and red volcanic debris, and loose rocks large as houses, ready on the slightest disturbance to roll down, crashing into the abysses below.
>
> On the summit of the island there floats almost constantly, even on the clearest day, a wreath of dense vapour, never still, but rolling and twisting into strange shapes as the wind eddies among the crags. And above this cloud-wreath rise mighty pinnacles of coal-black rock like the spires of some gigantic Gothic cathedral piercing the blue southern sky.
>
> As a consequence of the recoil of the rollers from the shore we found that, as we got nearer in, the ocean swell under us increased in height, and rose and fell in an uneasy confused fashion. The breakers were dashing up the cliffs with an ominous roar, showing us that, in all probability, landing would be out of the question for the present.

They eventually found a landing place and set up camp near South-West Bay where the treasure was allegedly buried. Sometimes they were able to leave *Alerte* at anchor, more often a sea crew had to jog her to and fro with her sails backed while the shore crew dug on.

The camp they erected was fenced to keep out the land crabs which skittered over every surface in a continual hunt for food. Knight was repelled by them:

> They swarm all over the place in incredible numbers. I have even seen them two or three deep in shady places under the rocks; they crawl over everything, polluting every stream, devouring anything – a loathsome lot of brutes, which were of use however, round our camp as scavengers. They have hard shells of a bright saffron colour, and their faces have a most cynical and diabolic expression. As one approaches them they stand on their hind legs and wave their pincers threateningly, while they roll their hideous goggle eyes at one in a dreadful manner. If a man is sleeping or sitting down quietly, these creatures will come up to have a bite at him, and would devour him if he was unable for some reason to shake them off; but we murdered so many in the vicinity of our camp during our stay that they certainly became less bold.

For three months the adventurers tunneled, dug and scraped for treasure. At one point the *Alerte* was almost lost on the rocks of Trinidad after her anchor dragged and the landing boats suffered damage coming in through the surf. Finally in February 1890 the exhausted treasure hunters threw in the towel, and, leaving only their broken wheelbarrows behind they sailed back to the River Thames via the Windward Islands where they enjoyed some rest and relaxation.

As to the treasure, Knight summarises thus:

> Knowing all I do, I have very little doubt that the story of the Russian Finn is substantially true – that the treasures of Lima were hidden on Trinidad; but whether they have been taken away, or whether they are still there and we failed to find them because we were not in possession of one link in the directions, I am unable to say.

NO WAY BACK: BY RAFT ACROSS THE PACIFIC

By bravely drifting 4 300 miles in a square-rigged balsawood raft, Thor Heyerdahl and his crew proved an ancient legend: that Polynesia's first visitors came from South America

Beneath the pitched roofs of a custom-made building a mouldering raft sits on plastic waves with dusty, model fish hanging beneath. Despite her rather forlorn appearance, such is the *Kon-Tiki* raft's grip on the imagination, that no less than 15 million people have visited her last resting place in Oslo, Norway, since she went on display in 1950.

On 28 April 1947, the *Kon-Tiki* was towed out of Callao harbour in Peru, and left to drift in the Humboldt Current her sails billowing in the strong trade wind. Her skipper was Thor Heyerdahl, who with his five-strong crew wanted to prove that the islands in the middle of the Pacific Ocean, collectively known as Polynesia, were inhabited by people from the far away continent of South America who had sailed there on giant balsa wood rafts. For over 100 years scientists had debated as to whether balsa rafts were seaworthy, and whether the Incas and their cultured predecessors, could have reached the islands out in the open Pacific.

Heyerdahl and his men did not know if the balsa logs would soak up so much sea water they would eventually become saturated and sink before they reached dry land. There was some evidence to show such rafts had made only coastal journeys in antiquity. At intervals, it was thought, they had been pulled up on the shoreline to dry out in the sun. Yet large sailing rafts were seen far out at sea and described in detail from 1526 and later by the pioneering Spaniards who first discovered and colonised the Pacific coast of South America. Small raft models, paddles and raft centreboards, have also been excavated in large numbers in graves along the coast of Peru and North Chile, some dating back, to the early centuries AD.

The *Kon-Tiki* raft was built of nine 2-foot-thick balsa logs, ranging in length from 30 to 45 feet, the longest in the middle, and lashed to balsa cross beams supporting a plaited bamboo deck and an open bamboo hut. Another worry was that the rope lashings would chafe as the logs moved about at sea. But as it turned out the lashings simply bit into the soft balsa logs and did not wear out. A bipod mast with a bamboo yard carrying a square sail; five centreboards thrust down in cracks between the logs; and a stout block of balsa supporting a long steering oar completed the construction. The *Kon-Tiki* was caught in two storms, one of which lasted for five days, but another bonus of the construction was that as waves broke on board they drained away immediately through the gaps between the logs. The raft was christened *Kon-Tiki*, after the legendary Sun-King from Inca history who ruled their land before the coming of the Incas, after which he migrated into the Pacific.

Every day the raft was driven westward and away from South America by the tradewind and the Humbolt Current, both of which maintained a steady course towards Polynesia. One thing the raft could not do was turn round and sail upwind against the prevailing trade winds which, with the current, helped her make up to 60 miles a day. She was like a 'cork steam-roller', Heyerdahl noted, which could not turn back. This meant that if anybody was lost over the side they could not be picked up. The ship's parrot was lost in this way and Herman Watzinger, the raft's meteorologist, went overboard and was only saved by the courage and quick-thinking of wireless operator Knut Haugland who dived in with a lifebelt on a line and swam to his shipmate. Both men were then hauled back aboard the disappearing raft.

Often, at dawn, edible flying fish and small squid would be found on deck and beneath the raft, dolphins, pilot fish, sharks, bonitos, and occasionally tuna fish, as well as edible plankton, swam in the shade. Rainwater was collected off the sail and liquid was squeezed from raw fish. The raft was also at various occasions visited by whales, and two specimens of the Gempylus or snake-mackerel, a fish which had never previously been seen alive by man, jumped aboard. On one occasion a whale-shark, the world's largest fish, kept up a vigil under the raft.

After 93 days at sea the expedition sighted land for the first time, but the raft could not be steered towards it and drifted helplessly past Puka-puka on the eastern fringe of the Tuamotu group. Four days later the *Kon-Tiki* passed so close to the island of Angatau that the natives ashore paddled out to the raft with their canoes, but once again she was swept past. At last after 101 days, and 4 300 miles (8 000 km) of the Pacific, the raft was caught in the surf and wrecked on the windward side of a coral reef just off the island of Raroia. But despite being shipwrecked Heyerdahl and his crew were jubilant: not only had they made it, they were well inside Polynesia and after a week they were found by native Polynesians who lived on the other side of the wide lagoon. The shallow raft eventually washed right over the reef and into the calm lagoon, where it was rescued, towed to Tahiti, and shipped back to Norway.

The documentary film of the story of the *Kon-Tiki* expedition won two Oscars in 1951 and Thor Heyerdahl's book *The Kon-Tiki Expedition* became an international best seller translated into nearly 70 languages.

THE QUEEN'S PIRATE

Francis Drake's plundering of the Spanish Men-of-War paid off England's debt and made this seafarer a national hero

One of 12 sons, Francis Drake grew up aboard an old naval hulk at Chatham on the River Medway and as a boy learned to sail in small boats on the Thames Estuary. At the age of 40 he sailed his ship the *Golden Hind* back up the river of his youth to be knighted by Queen Elizabeth I at Deptford. He was by now a millionaire, had his own coat of arms and the status of being the first Englishman to sail around the world.

It was the pinnacle of an astonishing rags to riches story which started with a slave-trading voyage to the Caribbean under John Hawkins. Having disposed of their human cargo: embarked on the west coast of Africa, the squadron of English ships docked at Spanish-held San Juan de Ulua in what is now Veracruz after being damaged in the tail end of a hurricane. The Spaniards guaranteed them safe harbour until the repair work was finished, and the ships victualled ready for the return home across the Atlantic. But the 'heretic' Protestants Hawkins and Drake were double-crossed by the Catholic Spaniards who attacked them, killing many of the party.

It was an act of treachery Drake never forgot and he returned in other ships to the Spanish Main and other parts of South America to sack and rob Spanish colonies.

His two-year circumnavigation was secretly sanctioned by Elizabeth who wanted the gold and silver being mined by the Spanish on the western seaboard of South America for England's coffers.

This entailed a three-ship convoy through the feared and unknown Magellan Strait at a time when simple folks believed the world was flat and the edge was somewhere south of the Canary Islands. Many of Drake's God-fearing sailors thought the Atlantic Ocean rushed ever faster the closer it got to the edge and pulled craft over into the abyss.

After losing two ships: one wrecked, the other returning to England, Drake battled on through the strait, successfully getting through to the Pacific. But then gale-force headwinds pushed him south of Cape Horn where he realised a passage around South America could be made in open water. It was two months after transiting the strait before he managed to reach Spanish settlements on the west side of the continent and start wreaking his revenge.

Eventually, laden with enough silver, gold, and other booty to help finance the home country for a year, and go towards the City of London's first institutions including banks, he sailed for home via the Philippines and the Cape of Good Hope.

He was a permanent thorn in the side of King Phillip II of Spain: sailing to Cadiz where he shot up the Spanish fleet 'singeing the King of Spain's beard' as the cavalier Drake put it.

In 1588 the greatest fleet the world had ever seen sailed up the English Channel under the command of Medina Sidonia. The Spanish Armada comprised nearly 130 ships with orders to make a bridgehead in the land of the heretics at either Dover or Margate depending on the wind direction. Admirals Drake, Howard, Hawkins and Frobisher chased and harried the Spanish all the way into the Dover Strait where, following a close brush with Drake's fire-ships, a north-westerly wind set some of the Armada onto the shoals off Gravelines and Ostend. Eventually the wind veered and the battered and disheartened Spanish sailed up the North Sea still chased by the English ships as far as Scotland. Happy that no landing was going to take place Drake and the other ship captains sailed home to the West Country leaving the Armada to sail around the treacherous waters north of Scotland. Many Spanish ships were lost at sea, others wrecked on the coasts of Scotland and Ireland. The invasion had become a total rout.

Years later when Drake returned to his quasi-official buccaneering on the Spanish Main he discovered the world had changed: mostly thanks to him. Spanish forts were more robustly built, their cannon were more accurate, and the locals – who once had assisted Drake – had been suppressed.

And, in 1596, on his last futile voyage of looting, he died after contracting dysentery and was buried at sea in a lead coffin off Puerto Bello, in what is now Venezuela.

SHOAL WATERS RUN DEEP

The smaller the boat the greater the adventure, runs the old saw: Charles Stock is living proof this is the case as he has sailed his 16-footer 70 000 miles in Home Waters: the equivalent of two circumnavigations

Micro-mariner Charles Stock, 82, has sailed 70 000 miles in his 16 ft gaffer, *Shoal Waters*, from Whitby to Poole. That's enough creek-crawling to make two circumnavigations. Because *Shoal Waters*, floats in 12 inches of water her owner uses two tenders to get out to her: one for each leg. His mud-spattered green wellie boots are almost as famous as his engine-less, green-hulled boat which has been a common sight on the waters of the East Coast and Solent over the last 45 years.

But it is not just in Britain's most popular cruising grounds that the little yacht's keel has sailed: Charles has cruised as far north as Whitby, across the North Sea to Belgium and France and as far west as Poole.

However, what really marks out the centre-boarder's passages are those which are not even covered by charts, in the canal-bound hinterland destinations of England's Home Counties. Many a dreamy commuter has done a double take when suddenly the fluttering of a sail has interrupted his reverie in Godalming, Bishop's Stortford, Guildford, Canterbury, Hertford and Chelmsford. He has crossed London's North Circular Road under all plain sail including topsail and once even sailed up a drain to get to Ilford.

'I keep a saw in the aft locker to cut away branches which block the boat's passage in upriver places', said the sailor, who keeps his boat on the River Blackwater near Maldon, Essex.

As you might expect from a former tax collector, Charles keeps tabs on everything including the construction of his boat: her interior lockers are made up from part of a billiard table, the top of a baby grand piano, and a section of an obsolete Lloyds Bank counter. The leather of the gaff jaws once held income tax papers, the compass came off an old D-Day landing craft, and the mast came from his first boat a rotten half-decker called *Zephyr* which he bought for £70 in 1951.

Charles sleeps in an 8 ft cabin and fires up a Gaz stove for a hot drink. He drinks from a china mug glazed with the St George's flag and was once a warm-up speaker for R.A. Butler, a minister in Winston Churchill's wartime government.

Two berths run each side of the centre-plate and have accommodated both Charles and his wife Joy over the years. Incredibly the couple even cruised with their four children: Priscilla, James, Penelope and Christopher in their early sailing years. A roomy cockpit tent helped out with the accommodation. But there is still only a bucket for a head. Fresh water is carried in two 10 gallon plastic jerrycans. Chain for the 17 lb fisherman's anchor drops into a bucket under the foredeck. Along the starboard cabin side a narrow shelf houses charts and a bottle of vodka. This is for injecting into the ancient brass steering compass when the air bubble gets too large to dampen the compass card.

The port quarterberth is blocked off to make space for the galley and stowage lockers. The deckhead is lined with polystyrene as an anti-condensation measure. *Shoal Waters*' pump is a sponge: she's never needed anything more complicated. Her depth sounder is two bamboo canes which lie along each side deck. Her lights run off a car battery, which is kept topped up with a detachable solar panel which sits on the cabin top but her riding light is still paraffin fuelled. She also has a quant pole so Charles can punt her along when in narrow shallow ditches, which is often. He will also don a harness and turn horse to tow her along if needs be: he once hauled her in this fashion 17 miles along canals to Basingstoke. She may sound primitive, but the little boat has served Charles well: he clocked up 3 147 miles in 1990 – his record cruising year – from Maldon to Dunkirk then to every creek in the Solent.

Charles does not believe in engines – he resents the capital and maintenance costs – and oily bilges.

The son of an East London gardener and a mother who was in domestic service: 'which sounds terrible but it certainly taught her how to cook: what I'd give now for some of my mum's rabbit pie', Charles was taken for days out at Southend's seaside aged eight. His first sail was in the old tripper boats: sloops which took people off the beach and around Southend Pier. 'They always went about so that whichever side you were sitting on you got the chance to trail your hand in the water,' he said.

Charles has never worn a lifejacket aboard *Shoal Waters* and his boat has never held flares. 'I regard everything on the boat from truck to keel as part and parcel of my safety equipment'.

Charles believes the most important safety factor is non-slip decks and he sprinkles fine sand on his freshly painted decks to give him a purchase.

His worst moment afloat was entering Blakeney Harbour in north Norfolk during an easterly gale. 'I was reefed right down and it was pretty terrifying. There was white water breaking everywhere and then suddenly I was over the bar and I could see grains of sand just a couple of feet beneath me. I found out later that the Coastguard had been watching my progress'.

FROM HONEYMOON TO SHIPWRECK

One of the virtues which helped this young Norwegian sailor survive a wedded life at sea was his sense of humour: he called the family pet dog Spare Provisions!

Romantic scribe Erling Tambs, 45, turned his life into a living poem by setting off in a 40 ft engineless cutter, the *Teddy*, with his young bride, Julie, on their honeymoon, before domestic bliss turned into the desire to make a circumnavigation.

Remarkably he covered much of his passages without using complete navigation, relying on dead reckoning alone: just measuring distance run and time elapsed. Many seamen of the past had done the same before the advent of the sextant and chronometer and Tambs had been at sea for eight years including time spent aboard square-riggers so he was a fine seaman if not the greatest navigator.

The honeymoon began in Oslo, capital of his native country, in August 1928. It was financed by a contract Tambs had acquired to write for a newspaper.

Teddy had an old compass, few charts, and no sextant, chronometer or nautical tables.

His North Sea chart was so old that Tambs could not recognise the lights of the Dutch coast and so stood close inshore in the hope of seeing a lightship and reading the name on her side. He sailed so close to the coastline that he even began to look for a road sign! Then an onshore storm blew up and *Teddy* had her first narrow escape almost piling up on the beach. Once back out in deep water Tambs reefed and hove-to. He lit the side lamps, and the exhausted couple slept for 14 hours during the storm.

Later Tambs steered too close to a Channel lightship and almost fouled one of her anchor buoys and they had a close encounter with a steamship which rocked their breakfast off the stove.

Tambs shook his fist at the steamer, but the skipper on the bridge mistook the gesture and gave him a friendly wave.

In the Bay of Biscay the voyage nearly ended in a total loss when the *Teddy*, sailing under reduced canvas at night, was almost run down by a barque, on the starboard tack.

Off the Portuguese coast he accidentally gybed, and broke the boom and he put into Vigo to make repairs. Here Tambs was given a dog born aboard a Norwegian ship, and he jokingly named her Spare Provisions. At first the dog was sea-sick, but by the time the yacht reached Lisbon she had got her sea legs.

Tambs bought a second-hand sextant at Lisbon and arrived in the Canary Islands via Madeira. Here his son, Tony, was born.

For his Atlantic crossing he had to rely on guesswork for his longitude as he did not have a chronometer, and his latitude was determined by noon sight.

But he sailed farther south than is usual, and when he thought he was near the South American coast he began to have doubts. He expected to see ships but saw none and instead found himself heading for the shoal water in the mouth of the River Orinoco. Tambs altered course to the north-west, and anchored at Curaçao, 48 days from the Canary Islands.

The tropical heat shrank the topside planks of the *Teddy* and she leaked badly so Tambs anchored at the island of Aruba, with two feet of water in the hold, but no cash to overhaul her. So Tambs earned money by giving a lecture. For seven weeks the *Teddy* was berthed on the Atlantic side of the Panama Canal awaiting a tow which he eventually managed. Tambs then sailed to Cocos Island, where he had a lucky escape from being marooned on the island. He had left his wife and child in the *Teddy* and went ashore in the dinghy for some coconuts. While ashore the dinghy painter chafed through on a rock and floated out to sea. Nervous of swimming because of sharks Tambs made a raft of saplings bound together with rope yarns from what was left of the painter. He poled towards the yacht, but he got into deep water where he could not reach the bottom, and the tide began to carry him past the yacht. He shouted, and the dog started to bark, waking Julie. Dashing on deck as her husband was being swept by, she seized a fishing line and threw an end to him. He grabbed it and pulled the frail raft towards the yacht. As soon as the raft hit the yacht's topsides it broke up. Tambs' first task was to sail after the dinghy, then he gave the dog a sumptuous meal to reinforce her guard-dog capabilities.

Teddy reached Nukuhiva from Cocos Island, in 45 days, but then hit more problems when Tambs broke the forestay on passage to Tahiti.

On passage from Samoa to New Zealand, the *Teddy's* crew all fell ill with influenza. Tambs poisoned his right hand, and the influenza caused complications, so for nearly three weeks the *Teddy* sailed herself across the Pacific, while Julie nursed her sick husband and tended her little son. On Christmas Eve Julie cried out that the yacht was surrounded by reefs which proved to be porpoises, and after this great relief Tambs' health began to improve.

They sailed into Auckland Harbour, New Zealand, without either charts or a pilot book. While in Auckland Julie gave birth to a daughter.

They eventually left for Brisbane, Australia, but the *Teddy* was becalmed and gripped by a strong current which carried her against the rocks on Challenger Island, in Hauraki Gulf, New Zealand.

Tambs jumped into the surf with son Tony in his arms and placed him on a ledge of rock above the surf and then returned to the yacht for his daughter. As Julie handed her over she slipped and fell into the surf between the yacht and the rocks. Tambs handed the baby to Tony, and then returned to save his wife.

Then the dog scampered out of the surf and Erling Tambs' remarkable voyage was over.

A BITTER-SWEET TASTE OF THE RACING LIFE

Covered in vomit, soaked to the skin and plagued with salt-water sores, cruising man Dick Durham tells of his introduction to ocean racing during the 2001 Fastnet Race

Hell is not fire and brimstone, but cold water and a lump of limestone four miles off the south-west coast of Ireland – I know because I've been there.

Even before I had left the Solent I was soaked to the skin, cold, hungry and contorted into an upright foetal position on the edge of a heeling boat. Earlier, at the start, Cowes had looked like a settlement in south-east Iceland as low-lying cloud was blown over it by a rising south-westerly Force 6. Some 250 boats, from 80-foot Maxis to family-owned 32-footers tacked back and forth off the Royal Yacht Squadron their heeling masts just feet from locking horns.

Before the Needles at least three boats had retired with broken running rigging (28 boats retired in all) and I prayed the 30-knot dead noser moaning through the steel rod calipers of our Bashford Howison 41's shrouds would buckle the rig enabling us to join the casualties.

But *Warpath* smashed manfully on, throwing salt-water in drenching showers over me and the seven others of us on watch. If the cold showers were all mine at least the £10 notes being torn up were the sponsor's – £25 000 no less, the sum a contact lens manufacturers had paid to have their name on the sails and to leave five of their employees on board for the benefit of character construction, begging for overtime rather than leave the warmth of the office ever again. Quite how they inserted their daily disposable contact lenses without poking their eyes out remains a mystery still.

It had all started earlier in the day as I chucked my kitbag aboard this modern racing hull and shivered as I noticed its bolt-on keel, dinghy-like hull and spade rudder. Racing sailor John Hanson, 30, gave us a briefing in the cockpit of *Warpath* which even the high banks of the River Hamble could not shelter from strong draughts of south-westerly dipping her shallow hull over and back as he spoke.

Hanson cheerfully explained the symptoms of hypothermia and got me to sign a piece of paper in which I accepted that 'ocean racing is a dangerous sport which can sometimes result in death or injury.'

As we came into the full force of the weather, unimpeded by the Isle of Wight, Ingo Boecker, a 34-year-old optician from Hamburg started whooping loudly like a kid at a fairground as *Warpath* rode through a series of switchback waves provided by the wind and the Shingles bank.

I am always made nervous by the naïve enthusiasm shown by novices confronted by rough weather: you just know Providence will want to teach them a lesson.

Suddenly and welcomingly I was hit by a warm wave. We must have crossed a shallow patch or an outfall, I mused, and licked my lips to remove the salt and instead located a small piece of ham which was strange as I had eaten only a cheese sandwich since leaving Cowes.

'I'm sorry,' gurgled a white-faced Boecker who was no longer cheering the waves.

'Come aft,' yelled Hanson from the cockpit.

'No I'm O.K.' a weakened Boecker replied.

'No you're not, get aft . . . downwind of me,' I shouted at him and the wretched fellow was sent below to nurse his sea-sickness.

Clear of the Needles Channel we had a rival on starboard – but not for long – *Moonduster*, a Frer 50-footer, skippered by wily octogenarian Denis Doyle, of the Royal Cork Yacht Club went about right under our lee and just ahead of us thereby forcing us – as the overtaking and windward boat to pinch up and consequently to lose speed and eventually drop under her lee.

But by now I could show little interest in the contest: the corporate oilskins I had been provided with were old and had seen better days. The zip fastener on the jacket had teeth which unpeeled leaving a hair-covered Velcro strip to unsuccessfully hold the lapels together. To compound my self-pity, I had discovered that all my spare clothing was soaked as well as that which I had on. My kit-bag had mysteriously jumped out of a bunk and into the slopping bilges.

Discomfort had reduced me to baseness: I judiciously lay down the useless oilskin among the mash of wet clothing below and crawled into a wet, nylon lee cloth. When I climbed back out I noticed the offending garment had gone: claimed by some other poor sap and I pulled on another. Success! The zip worked.

So now, I apologize, to whichever of you, my fellow crew members, got lumbered.

Later in a fit of guilt I admitted my crime to Hanson.

'Bloody great and here I am trying to build team spirit,' he said.

24 hours later – 18 of those spent in exhaustion on the rail – I blinked myopically at what somebody told me was Start Point. I could not have cared if it was Cape Horn. Nobody in ocean racing, it seemed, drank hot drinks or ate hot meals. They lived, instead, on pre-packed sarnies, revolting high energy glucose drinks and bottled water.

My role, in this team effort, was as a 12-stone lump of human ballast, up on that damned aluminium toe-rail, the countersunk screw-heads of which had formed indents in my backside. That toe-rail was the frontline: going over the top of which was the poor bloody infantry of the ocean race. The frontline was the place all of us had to perch when going 'uphill'. I watched my counterparts pass on other boats clinging like gaily coloured parasites to the gleaming whale-like hulls.

Back up I went to hang between the top wire and the padded bottom wire of the guard rails, as though on a yard arm. Now at least I will always know who the racing nutters are: theirs are the boats with the padded bottom wire.

Soon my hood was pulled back over my head and with the others I telescoped my neck like a pigeon dozing on a high city parapet.

Humped next to Jean Accad, 40, from Paris, I found myself listening to a reverie of beautiful cruising in Brittany as the poor man, apparently semi-delirious, recalled his normal sailing days as a form of escapism.

And so life formed a dreary routine: six hours on, three off.

The three off were almost as bad as the six on. I climbed into a damp, plastic cave-like quarter berth where I could smell the previous occupant.

These racing boyos don't even give you warning when they are putting about. There's none of the gentlemanly 'Ready about', 'Lee-o' we cruising folks are used to. Instead they use the much more urgent; 'Tack, 3-2-1' and bosh, you are on the other tack. I tried to clamber out of my berth while the boat was upright, as once she was over on her ear it was a painful climb. My soaking wet gloves snagged the Velcro strips laid bare by the removal of the saloon cushions: a wimpish cruising luxury thrown out to make room for more sails.

Nighttime and very poor visibility off the Bishop's Rock had me wondering about 32-year-old navigator Duncan Barr's accuracy. He had told me earlier he had never gone offshore before but was an experienced dinghy sailor.

Why oh why wasn't I anchored under the lee of some East Coast shoal, with a mug of tea, the cabin lamp illuminating a good book and a warm sleeping bag?

I need not have worried however, Barr proved to be a superb yachtsman and next day as we headed out into the Irish Sea I asked another top sailor, Fastnet four-timer and Round Ireland Race winner Michael Boyd, a 50-year-old businessman, if we were anywhere near the Labadie Bank.

'It will be signposted when we get to it,' teased the charming Dubliner.

Hanson talked of the US tornados which are 'dumped' in the Fastnet area by southerly, shifting jet streams in August. 'It's part of the Fastnet mystique,' he said.

Another journalist on the boat, ashen-faced Lionel Bret from the Paris office of laddish magazine *FHM*, looked more like the representative of *Funeral Directors' Monthly*. He told me he would rather be climbing in the mountains of his boyhood Grenoble.

'Relax,' I said trying to reassure him, 'out here the boat will do the climbing.'

By now the boat below was like a U-Boat which had been submerged at sea for three months.

Bilge water ran over the sole between sodden sailbags which made a visit to the heads an undulating moon walk. From the deckhead grab rails hung wet dripping harnesses. Oilskins hung swinging and dripping. Beads of water ran down the lining, body heat caused condensation. Old crisp bags, empty tins of Red Devil, crushed plastic mineral water bottles, scraps of chocolate bar foil and missing socks were everywhere. The whole was covered by a clammy, fuggy smell of vile bodies.

After 36 hours I could not hang onto the contents of my bladder any longer and I crawled to the heads, kneeled on the cabin sole and aimed my shrivelled, salt-water enfeebled manhood into the heads: anywhere into the heads, but at least over the threshold of the heads. I sponged up the result and squeezed it into the water closet. It hardly seemed worth the effort just to make room for another slug of mineral water. I would have given six month's salary for a sudden coronary and the subsequent airlift to a warm bed, a fussing nurse and a cup of tea.

Skipper John 'Fish' Fisher, 31, is a taciturn, but consummate yachtsman, an intuitive seaman. He took care of any fear factor and left me instead to indulge myself in my misery of dampness and, after two days, terribly painful sores around my nether regions from salt water and the 'frontline.'

From Land's End our south-westerly had provided us with a fast reach which dropped as suddenly 'as though the 50p ran out in the hair dryer,' as Hanson put it, leaving us rolling in airless seas 30 miles from the Rock. Then out of the mist appeared *Moonduster*. We headed north for, according to Boyd, 'the whoosh of the tide along the coast on the making tack.' *Moonduster*, ominously, headed south.

Five hours later we rounded the majestic rock which sat like a Gothic castle on a gently swollen sea. The sunset loomed behind south-west Ireland like napalm – the low, crumbling cumulus below the orange horizon like a burning Vietnamese treeline.

There was no sign of *Moonduster* – for company rounding the Fastnet Rock we had *Independent Bear*.

'You're about 15 minutes in a RIB from the best fish food in Ireland there at Baltimore,' mocked Boyd.

Now, at last, the voyage on Das Boot without the depth charges was over. The boat was upright and I fell asleep in the downed genoa as the spinnaker tugged us along through a star-lit night as dolphins bathed in the green and red navigation lights.

I plucked up the courage to remove my feet from my seaboots: they appeared to be as though freshly unwrapped from a recently exhumed mummy. The tart aroma from the boots themselves corresponded with the first fumes coming from an opened tomb discovered after millenia.

'Coo they stink,' said Gill Perkins, 29, the only female member of the crew, as I sheepishly handed them up for an airing. I decided to plunge the offending digits into my virgin deck shoes purchased especially for, but so far unused in the Fastnet.

Perkins had become a mass of bruises. She had fallen, collided, tripped and walked into every dimension the boat had to offer. She had ignored Hanson's briefing: one hand for yourself and one for the boat and instead sacrificed every limb to *Warpath*.

But even now we were upright there was no let up from our racing masters. For downwind sailing means trimming the spinnaker. And it was 'grind' if banker Niall Dowling, 24, was the trimmer or 'wind' if Hanson was in charge. Either way that damned kite had to be trimmed all day and all night all the way back to Plymouth.

But at least I had dried out some clothes. At least the sun had come out. Best of all Fisher had actually got the gas stove to work and made me a cup of tea.

Exactly 24 hours after rounding the Fastnet we breasted the Bishops Rock light again, this time leaving it to the north of us instead of to the south.

A mystery yacht glided next to us in the night. Was it *Moonduster*? We couldn't tell. Shooting stars fell to earth and slowly the Lizard lighthouse darted a reptilian-like tongue of light into the night sky.

Three days and 19 hours after leaving Cowes we got the Royal Ocean Racing Club hooter at Plymouth Breakwater. *Moonduster* was moored up and deserted when we motored into Queen's Battery Marina. Overall *Moonduster* came 23rd and *Warpath* 47th. In class *Moonduster* was 10th and *Warpath* 17th.

Of *Warpath's* racing novices Andrew MacDonald, 49, swore he would never step foot on a racing boat again but will consider cruising; so too did Ingo, but he is to learn how to sail in order to go cruising; Perkins said she wanted to explore the Med in a cruising boat and Accad said he would never consider a Fastnet again, but would continue cruising in Britanny.

Hanson, Fish, Dowling, Boyd and bowman Peter 'Chopper' Simon, 25, are all Fastnet veterans and ever-ready for more offshore racing.

As for me I'm a convert. The boat I had doubted was in fact, fast, strong and seaworthy. And although ocean racing is one of those things that's great when it is over, it is an experience in which you make lasting and good friends.

I will never forget the friendly rub across the back Fish gave me as I wrote up my log on the chart table. It meant I had been accepted and coming from a seaman of his calibre was praise indeed.

DAYBOAT CAPSIZE, GALES AND DISMASTING

Frank Dye became a legend after sailing a Wayfarer dinghy to Iceland. His legacy lives on as people follow in his wake making cruising passages in open boats

In July 1963 a 16 ft Wayfarer sailing dinghy, *Wanderer*, set out from Kinlochbervie in Sutherland on the west coast of Scotland with two men aboard. The forecast, southerly Force 6–7 had much larger boats seeking shelter. Frank Dye, a car salesman, was the skipper and an RAF corporal Russell Brockbank, the crew and they were about to make small-boat history.

Armed with just a compass and sextant for navigation and with a makeshift cockpit tent for shelter, they headed out to sea and within hours were hove-to, putting in reefs and during the first night Brockbank, a novice sailor, was violently seasick.

The following day the wind was even stronger and they dropped the sails and then lowered the mast, removed the rudder and paid out a sea anchor. For 12 hours they lay in soaked clothing before the wind eased enough to step the mast once more and under heavily reefed mainsail they got under way. But later that day the wind increased to Force 7 again and they had to lower the mast for the second time.

Day three saw them riding a huge swell in very little wind which gave them a chance to strip off their sodden clothing and rig them up to dry. The wind backed to the north-east and soon they were planing in a Force 5.

Seven days out they were forced to lower the mast again and deploy the sea anchor as they were hit by a Force 8 gale which kept them shivering under the boat cover for 20 hours. That night they alternately reefed sail in a squall, then dropped out the reefs as the blow passed; bailed out the dinghy, then put the reefs in again as another squall hit them with freezing temperatures.

At last the wind eased and became steady and under full sail they continued, but while Dye was 'off watch' and asleep the starboard shroud broke, fortunately the quick-thinking Brockbank put the boat on the port tack although this shroud was bent.

After 11 days they managed to get into Heimay, an island which is part of Iceland.

On his second major sea passage, a Norwegian Sea crossing from Scotland to Aalesund, Norway, Dye and his crew, narrowly survived four capsizes and a broken mast during a Force 9 storm. Dye later described the conditions: 'It was impossible to look into the wind. It was screaming and the tops of the waves were blown completely away, feeling like hail. Within our limited vision the whole sea seemed to be smoking. Just to see such seas break away on the beam was frightening – 25 ft of solid water, with another 12 ft of overhanging crest above it. It was only a matter of time before we got one aboard'.

Wanderer limped into Aalesund under jury rig.

Dye's Norfolk-built boat logged tens of thousands of miles and after shipping her to the USA in 1988, he survived a hurricane while sailing alone in the North Atlantic.

'Offshore cruising in an open boat can be hard, cold, wet, lonely and occasionally miserable,' Dye wrote, 'but it is exhilarating too. To see the beauty of dawn creep across the ever restless and dangerous ocean; to make a safe landfall – is wonderful and all of these things develop a self-reliance that is missing from the modern, mechanical, safety-conscious civilised world'.

At the 1963 Earl's Court Boat Show he met a dinghy sailor called Margaret, who decided to marry him the following year, even though she had been warned not to sail with 'that man; he'll kill you'.

Their honeymoon was spent voyaging to the remote uninhabited Hebridean island of St Kilda; their wedding breakfast consisted of 'green pea soup and scrambled eggs' served in an insulated mug. Margaret said despite wearing many layers of clothing, 'never before had I known what it was like to be so cold'. But she went on to sail with her husband for 30 years.

With his wife, Dye began the tradition of Wayfarer cruising rallies. His exploits also earned him a place in the National Maritime Museum at Falmouth, in a display entitled 'Endurance and Survival'. *Wanderer* is now on permanent display at the museum.

RECORD OF RECORDS

Tristan Jones was determined to set a new record in sailing: to voyage on the lowest water in the world and the highest

Man has long seen the ocean as a challenge, but the mania for using the watery three-quarters of planet earth for breaking records is a comparatively new phenomenon. As the late 20th century saw men and women driven to sea to be the first in ever more bizarre challenges, one yachtsman came up with the strangest quest of all: to sail on the highest and lowest water in the world. With a brilliant sense of originality, not to say parody, characteristic of the man, Tristan Jones, said: 'I would set a record that will not be broken until man finds water amongst the stars'.

In 1970 the Welsh-born ocean-going sailor and author arrived at Haifa, Israel in a 38 ft yawl *Barbara*, borrowed from an American benefactor Arthur Cohen. Here she was hauled out, put on an Israeli tank-transporter left over from the Six-Day War and driven across the desert to the Dead Sea – the 47-mile long, 10-mile wide salty lake between Israel and Jordan which is 1 250 feet below sea level. The boat was re-launched into the eerie oasis at En Gedi and Jones sailed her south to the Biblical ruins of Sodom. He used an outboard engine to motor back to En Gedi and had her hauled out again for a road journey to Eilat and the Red Sea.

Jones then sailed down the Indian Ocean, around the Cape of Good Hope and across the Atlantic to Recife, Brazil and eventually up the Amazon to a point above Manaus, which in 1972 was the furthest a yacht had been sailed up that tropical river.

From there he sailed to the Caribbean and the Virgin Islands, and returned *Barbara* to her owner. Under Jones' two and a half year captaincy she had sailed 38 000 miles.

Now the bearded explorer bought *Sea Dart*, a Debutante, a 17 ft, plywood bilge keeler and sailed her to Panama, transited the canal and coasted down to Callao the port of Lima, Peru.

It was now December 1973 and the indefatigable Jones was disheartened when he discovered he faced a fight with daunting red tape to be able to take his boat overland to Lake Titicaca: 'South American bureaucracy, just about the worst in the world – a continual Mad Hatter's tea party, a crazy blizzard of paperwork, a marathon of marching in the heat from one dingy office to another, from one garlic-breathed manipulator of paper clips to the next'.

But he won the fight and on New Year's Day 1974, *Sea Dart* was launched into the Peruvian waters of the lake 12 850 feet above sea level. He ran aground on a 'shoal' of underwater trees, helped the local Uros Indians – who live on eyeless toads found at the bottom of the lake – reclaim their land: a floating mass of vegetation which had broken adrift in a storm, and gained a young pilot – Huanapaco – to help him navigate and spent six weeks cruising in Peru. At night they would simply 'run aground' in reed beds where they were held fast by the stalks until morning.

When he sailed into Bolivian waters to the port of Tiquina where there is a naval base, he was arrested and jailed because the young marines thought his red ensign was a communist flag: and that Inglaterra was a port in Peru!

Huanapaco, who had temporarily disembarked from *Sea Dart* earlier to visit his family, arrived to save the day, bringing with him a Bolivian naval officer who secured Jones' release.

Now Jones made plans to get his boat back to the open sea. This entailed shipping her by rail across the Chaco Desert to the Brazilian frontier in the state of Mato Grosso and then take her 2 000 miles down the River Paraguay to the Plate estuary.

He had her lifted out in Guaqui and onto a giant truck which slid off the icy road to La Paz, twice and sat at an 80 degree angle for two days awaiting a haul out from a tractor. They eventually crossed the Andes and went from freezing snow and ice to 120 degree heat on the Chaco plains where *Sea Dart* was loaded onto a train and taken across the desert to a frontier town: Puerto Suarez, but this place was 16 miles from the river.

So Jones and his trusty companion spent 21 days hauling her there by hand with a block and tackle and a 'road' of well-greased railway sleepers which they laid and re-laid as she headed east. Apart from the gargantuan task of the labour Jones was dogged by the nagging fear that the river waters were dropping too rapidly to be able to float *Sea Dart* when he arrived.

When they got to the river the jetty they hoped to use to launch her was rotted to dust and the old steam crane which could have lifted her was a pile of rust. So for eight days the pair slashed down bushes, moved stones and dug the earth away until they had built a slipway!

At last they were able to launch *Sea Dart* and they sailed her through a 'green hell' of jungle – taking the boat up wrong turns and dead ends and having to haul her back against the stream. They used burning strands of rope to keep the leeches at bay as they jumped overboard to drag her back into the main stream and also braved snakes and piranha. Three weeks they spent in the Mato Grosso 'nature gone wild – a mad biological riot' with 'millions' of insects descending on them every minute. It was, Jones said, 'a rotting, evil malignant inferno'.

Both men were riddled with tapeworm, but at last they sailed into the main stream of the River Paraguay and now faced the rapids at Paso de Moros, bumping the boat's three bilge keels 20 times over the flat stones as the torrent swept them through.

At Coimbra they rested up and then continued out of Brazil and into Paraguay arriving in Ascuncion in late November and Buenos Aires by December and finally Montevideo.

From there Jones came back to England where, penniless, he slept under a tree on Hampstead Heath! He went back to his old job working in the boiler room at Harrods and prepared for his next adventure.

PART SIX

Tragedy

THE LAST TRAGIC VOYAGE OF FRANCIS CHICHESTER

He was a national hero, knighted by the Queen, but a lone sailor. Francis Chichester's last voyage was a venture tainted with death and failure

More than half a million people lined the shores of Plymouth Sound to greet Francis Chichester and his 53 ft ketch, *Gipsy Moth IV*, back from his solo circumnavigation of the world on 28 May 1967. Queen Elizabeth II knighted him at Greenwich for the feat, dubbing him with Sir Francis Drake's sword. Chichester was not the first man to sail around the world alone, but he had been the fastest: covering more than 29 500 miles in a sailing time of 226 days. And it was speed that had made his name in the sailing world when he won the first single-handed transatlantic race in 1960 in *Gipsy Moth III*. The name *Gipsy Moth* came from his original attempt at speed records in a plane of the same name. He had hoped to fly solo around the world in a Gipsy Moth plane, but the bid almost killed him when he crashed in Japan having hit telephone wires.

But his last voyage was the very opposite of triumph. It ended in tragedy, which although only indirectly connected with Chichester himself, left the nation's hero being severely criticised in the press.

This wiry, resourceful adventurer could never resist a challenge and aged 71 and in ill-health he set off again from Plymouth in the 1972 edition of the solo transatlantic race in *Gipsy Moth V*, a 57 ft ketch designed by Robert Clark. Everyone was rooting for the world's most famous sailor and after two days of gales other contestants started retiring. Not so Chichester. But no-one could know how ill he was as his ageing Mark II Marconi radio had refused to transmit in the first few days of the race and alone on board the constant battering of wind and sea was taking its toll. In his log he recorded: 'I must lay down 10 min. every hour. I carry a cockpit half mattress and it saves me from pressing bones against sharp edges and corners.'

Chichester had beaten off cancer 14 years before with a combination of natural remedies and prayer. Now, six days out, it had returned with a vengeance and as the heavy weather brought on increased agony he took a dose of pain killers and went into a heavy sleep. When he came round he did not know if he had been asleep for a few hours or a few days and so for the first time in his life he decided to quit. After eight days in the race he turned *Gipsy Moth V* round and headed for home.

His rogue radio was still receiving and as Chichester headed back to the busy Western Approaches he repeatedly heard Portishead Radio asking him to make contact. Newspapers ran headlines like: 'Fears for Sir Francis after Radio Silence', 'Growing Concern over Chichester'. And RAF planes on training flights now had a real life exercise: trying to locate the 'missing' Chichester. Then on 27 June a merchant ship the *SS Barrister* spotted *Gipsy Moth V* halfway between the Azores and Land's End and reported her position to Lloyd's of London, the shipping news bulletin.

The ship's report included the news that *Gipsy Moth V* was heading towards America which meant she appeared to be lagging uncharacteristically behind. In fact Chichester was just making a tack at the time which made it appear he was heading west when in fact he was heading for Plymouth. Now the RAF planes could find him but they saw that he was heading east. New headlines screamed: 'Where is he Going?'; 'New Riddle'.

Next a low flying Nimrod used lamp signals to ask if he was OK. Chichester lamped back: 'I have been ill.' The Nimrod asked if he needed help. Chichester signalled back: 'I am OK. No rescue!'. The following day a second Nimrod received the signal: 'Wish son and Anderson could meet me in Channel.' John Anderson was a newspaperman who understood sailing and had become a friend of Chichester's following the coverage of his circumnavigation. In a second message Chichester had signalled: 'Weak and Cold. Want rest'. The message was misinterpreted as: 'Want Brest.' The Nimrod then suggested that ships in the vicinity might like to check out the situation and this was heard by a French weather ship *France II*, which steamed to the position given and located Chichester who signalled: 'No aid needed. Thank you. Go away.'

Before she did so the *France II* was in collision with *Gipsy Moth V* damaging her mizzen mast which later snapped in two. Now *HMS Salisbury* had been diverted from exercises to find Chichester and offer assistance if required. Chichester's son Giles and John Anderson has been dropped on board by helicopter. Three seamen and Giles boarded *Gipsy Moth V* via an inflatable dinghy and helped Chichester into Plymouth where he was hospitalised.

Now the peculiar psyche of English tradition turned on its hero. Winners are OK but losers pose questions and one MP asked questions in Parliament about the cost to the public of the 'recent air-sea rescue of Sir Francis Chichester.' But being accused of using taxpayer's money was nothing to what happened next. Twelve hours after leaving *Gipsy Moth V*, the weather ship *France II* had collided with an American yacht *Lefteria*. The yacht sank with the loss of seven of her 11 crew. The four survivors were taken to La Rochelle on the weather ship and as news leaked out press reports incorrectly stated that both the *France II* and the yacht had gone to the aid of *Gipsy Moth IV*. This was soon followed with uninformed comment blaming Chichester for the tragedy, accusing him of irresponsibility by setting off on an ocean voyage while unfit, refusing assistance in an offhand manner, and endangering people's lives.

Chichester explained in print that he was in no way responsible for the tragedy and the surviving crew of the *Lefteria*, an 80-year-old schooner, confirmed that they were not en route to *Gipsy* M*o*th *V's* aid, but in fact on passage to the West Indies. But this did not make such large headlines.

Chichester died from a cancerous tumour on the spine two months after arriving back at Plymouth.

SAILING INTO MADNESS

Damned by certain shipwreck if he sailed on and damned with financial ruin if he turned back, perhaps the desperate Donald Crowhurst found another way out

Simon Crowhurst was eight years old when he waved a final farewell to his father and watched a lone figure sail into a cold, grey English Channel aboard his 40 ft plywood, ketch-rigged trimaran *Teignmouth Electron*. It was the last day of October and the last day of the deadline for those entering the *Sunday Times* Golden Globe Race. Fellow competitors Chay Blyth, Robin Knox-Johnston and John Ridgeway had all sailed off in June, while Frenchman Bernard Moitessier and Bill King left Plymouth in August.

Crowhurst, a 36-year-old electronics engineer, was the dark horse in the race who would go on to steal the show for all the wrong reasons. Simon was with his mother Clare, and brothers, James, Roger and sister Rachel, as he watched his father's boat towed over the start line to begin his epic voyage. From the very beginning, Donald Crowhurst faced insurmountable problems. As the last of his last-minute supplies were tossed aboard *Teignmouth Electron*, he couldn't hoist his foresails, because a rubber masthead buoyancy bag fouled the halyards. The jib and staysail had also been attached to the wrong stays.

Accompanied by a mini-flotilla of three motorboats with 40 friends and the BBC aboard, Donald Crowhurst shouted in jest: 'I'll be glad when I'm on my own without help from you bloody lot!' and asked for a tow back to harbour. He then reportedly gave his wife, Clare, a reassuring wink.

Some 90 minutes later he set off again, tacking out into Lyme Bay and finally disappearing forever into the murky rain and fading light as dusk came. A vital bag of spares, including rigging screws and pipe for the bilge pumps, had been left ashore. Simon, now 47, struggles to reconcile his memory of that poignant afternoon with photographs of *Teignmouth Electron* now lying in her final resting place, sun-bleached and forgotten on the shoreline of the Caribbean island of Cayman Brac.

Eight months and ten days after leaving Devon, the trimaran was found drifting in mid-Atlantic with no sign of her skipper. The battered hulk was lifted aboard a ship and is now all that remains of a great adventure which turned into a deadly trap for his father.

'I have mixed feelings about that boat,' said Simon, a scientific researcher at Cambridge University. 'My father seriously considered not taking delivery of her. In the rush to get her ready for the race, serious short cuts were made in her construction'. Although the hulls had been sheathed in fibreglass they ran out of time to sheath the decks which, instead, were painted. 'My father was furious when he found out. Later, the hull split, partly because of this structural defect'.

Crowhurst, who had no experience of multihull sailing, set off in a boat that was not seaworthy. On day five he noticed bubbles blowing out of the hatch on the bow of the port hull. He opened it to find the hull flooded to deck level. The genoa track was lifting off the deck and he had virtually no spare screws. More demoralisingly, his Marconi radio transmitter wasn't working.

'Even as a child, I could see it was a muddle before he left. You don't set off for a voyage around the world in that state. There were systematic faults with the boat which couldn't be sorted out once he had put to sea,' said Simon.

The night before his departure Donald Crowhurst voiced his doubts to his wife Clare. After rowing out to the boat for a final inspection, they sorted out as much as they could of the piled-up equipment and went back to the hotel at 2am.

As they lay in bed, Donald reportedly asked Clare: 'Darling, I'm very disappointed in the boat . . . if I leave with things in this hopeless state will you go out of your mind with worry?'

Clare replied with another question: 'If you give up now will you be unhappy for the rest of your life?'

Donald didn't answer, but started to cry. He wept until dawn. 'I was such a fool!' Clare said months later. 'I didn't realize Don was telling me he'd failed and wanted me to stop him. He'd always been so brilliant at making things come right in a crisis that I never imagined he couldn't do it again'.

'The momentum had built up,' said Simon. 'People were egging my father on. Even though he had serious misgivings, it was very difficult to pull back from the brink'. Simon believes his father could have retired after a fortnight. 'It would have been embarrassing, but he still would have been one of the competitors in the *Sunday Times* race and it would have given him a platform for launching his Navicator' (Crowhurst's radio-direction finder invention).

Crowhurst's doubts about his boat's readiness were brushed aside by his sponsor, Stanley Best, who had paid the £12 000 boat-building bill. His press agent Rodney Hallworth, an ex-*Daily Mail* reporter, told him he must go. Crowhurst had been 'sold' to the public as the brave amateur yachtsman pitted against more seasoned sailors. If successful, he stood to win a £5 000 prize, worth £60 000 in today's money.

Two weeks after setting off, Crowhurst made a list of the boat's defects and *did* consider giving up. His cockpit hatch leaked so badly it flooded the generator. All three hulls were leaking and 17 days after leaving he bailed 150 gallons of water out of the hulls. With no radio he had no time signals and his chronometer was useless.

One vital factor forcing him to carry on was that he had signed a contract to buy the boat if anything went wrong with the voyage. This would almost have certainly bankrupted his business. Faced with financial ruin if he turned back, the intrepid Crowhurst carried on.

Sometime in December he came to a fateful decision. His log book no longer recorded the normal daily, sometimes hourly comments about speed, sea state and course. Instead, page after page showed neatly pencilled mathematical calculations of his sextant sights.

Early in December he claimed a new 24-hour record for a solo sailor of 243 miles. Francis Chichester, one of the race advisers, was sceptical and said Crowhurst had to be 'a bit of a joker'.

Crowhurst started a second logbook, in which he kept track of his actual positions. In the original logbook, he plotted a carefully detailed series of fake positions each day, placing *Teignmouth Electron* further and further from her actual position.

Becalmed in the doldrums and caught in an ordinary tropical rain squall, he cabled Rodney Halworth to say that a 45 knot line squall had smashed the windvane. Later he cabled that he was averaging 170 miles daily when his a true distance that day was 13 miles.

On Christmas Eve he called Clare and said he was 'somewhere off Cape Town' when, in fact, he was 20 miles from the Brazilian coast. By now Moitessier was in sight of New Zealand's south island and Knox-Johnston was battling across the Southern Ocean towards Cape Horn.

In January, Cape Town radio tried repeatedly to transmit a cable to Crowhurst from Stanley Best saying he was waiving the boat's repurchase clause. Crowhurst could return without facing ruin. But with supreme irony, Crowhurst was maintaining radio silence as part of his deception. He never responded.

While Crowhurst was reported to be 'limping on after a battering by a giant wave' in the Indian Ocean, he was, in fact, still mid-Atlantic bailing his leaky hull. He spent most of January and February zigzagging off the coasts of Brazil and Uruguay with daily distances of 20–30 miles.

Then on 6 March his non-stop voyage suddenly ended when he made a secret landing at Rio Salado, Argentina, where he dropped anchor. He soon went aground on a sandbank under the nose of the local Coastguard Station. But Rio Salado was a sleepy village with a dirt road and no telephones. His arrival was officially recorded but never discovered until months later.

Crowhurst, dressed in red shirt, khaki shorts and with a scraggly beard, pointed out his damaged hull to the locals and spent the next day repairing the leaks with two plywood patches and other materials given to him. Two days later he set sail.

In 16 000 miles of sailing, Crowhurst had never left the Atlantic. His plan was to let his fellow competitors get ahead so he could tag on as tail-end Charlie, thus ensuring that his log books would not be scrutinised.

On 9 April Crowhurst broke radio silence to report he was heading to Diego Ramirez, an island south-west of Cape Horn. Most of Fleet Street bought the con, but Francis Chichester expressed concerns to race officials.

By now only two other boats were left in the race: Knox-Johnston's *Suhaili* was a day away from arriving in Falmouth. But after 319 days at sea, would his time be fast enough to win the £5 000 prize for the fastest circumnavigation?

Nigel Tetley's trimaran, *Victress,* a sister ship to *Teignmouth Electron*, was close to the Azores. Considering Crowhurst had left the UK six weeks after him, Tetley was surprised at Crowhurst's rapid progress. Estimating he was just two weeks ahead of his rival, Tetley drove his boat hard through a storm, desperate to stay in front. But *Victress* was also leaking and just 1 200 miles from the finish she broke up. Tetley watched from his life-raft as she vanished beneath the waves, together with all his hopes.

Hearing about Tetley's rescue in a cable from Clare, Crowhurst realised he now couldn't avoid the full glare of the media spotlight as the prize winner of the fastest circumnavigation.

'My father was someone who thought of all the angles and to some extent what he did was the typical gambler's strategy. You lose one bet, so you raise the stakes. He was a naturally optimistic person. But when the news came through about Tetley, I believe that's when he started to deteriorate,' said Simon.

Crowhurst spent the next month mulling over his predicament and trying to escape the consequences by retreating into his log books, which had become more metaphysical than maritime.

'His writings became an extended soliloquy on the subject of death,' said Simon. 'At the end there's a terrible clarity, a decisiveness, to them. The phrase he used "IT IS THE MERCY" echoes the last words of Jesus on the cross. Time had become something of cosmic significance. He felt he was leaving a valuable insight – that this would offset what he'd suffered already – he was at peace in one sense'.

On 23 June 1969 Simon believes his father stepped off *Teignmouth Electron* holding his chronometer and the false log book and drowned himself.

'Certainly there are worse ways to go . . . I hope it wasn't too bad for him'.

The Crowhurst family suffered a 'huge emotional roller coaster' during the voyage: first the weeks of radio silence, then the sudden news that Donald was set to win the race, followed by the discovery of the abandoned boat and the news that he'd faked his entire voyage. 'For months there were reports of dad being seen in other parts of the world, like Lord Lucan,' said Simon, 'it was a nightmare'.

'My mother is still traumatised by it all. She, as well as my brother and sister still suffer deep wounds from it all. We all have differences of opinion as to what happened, but we were all loyal to my father'.

Gallantly, Robin Knox-Johnston donated his £5 000 winner's prize money to the Crowhurst family. It helped them keep their Devon home.

'Robin Knox-Johnston is a real hero,' said Simon.

In the 1960s Britain expected a lot from her heroes. In 1967 Francis Chichester's solo round the world voyage in *Gipsy Moth IV* was said to have restored Britain's mastery of the Seven Seas. It was the stiff upper lip against a backdrop of free love, hippies and flower power. In today's celebrity-sated society, Donald Crowhurst would never have endured the same stigma of 'failure'.

'Today he would have survived,' said Simon, 'TV adventurers stay in hotels when they are supposed to be roughing it in the wilds. Then there was a lady walking round the world who took lifts in cars. People have a more realistic idea of how humans behave under extreme pressure. We are more cynical, yes, but we are wiser. Hopefully if my father has contributed anything then it's to a better understanding of the human limits of endurance and what happens when people fail. Maybe that has helped others survive. I certainly hope so'.

Of the boat Simon said: 'She is decaying rather gracefully. I think the next hurricane will probably destroy what's left of her. I've thought of going out to Cayman Brac . . . it would be a kind of pilgrimage . . . not that dad was a saint!'

AFTER THE WAVE

The 2004 Boxing Day tsunami which claimed more than 280 000 lives, was dubbed the 'worst natural disaster in history'. Thailand, a popular yacht-charter destination was one of the countries hit hard. Dick Durham took the first charter after the waves receded

Red ribbons flutter from the stems of boats in Thailand in honour of Buddha. Garlands of flowers are added for good luck. But not even the enlightened one could offer protection from the earth's indifferent flexing of her tectonic muscles. Thousands of lives were lost and fishing boats, tourist craft and yachts were tossed into the jungle, sunk or mashed on the reefs of Thailand's west coast when the Boxing Day earthquake sent in 10-metre waves. Yet what Buddha did supply to the citizens of this stunning country was a stoicism of spirit that we from the chilly and secular West can only wonder at.

It is 5 o'clock on Friday afternoon at the Watermark bar in the Boat Lagoon on the east coast of Phuket island and 'happy hour' has just started. As a tyrannical sun drops behind the jungle of the hinterland, yachtsmen gather to talk of the week just past. Even though they are sinking two beers for the price of one the conversation is muted. It is five weeks since the Boxing Day tsunami crashed ashore, but the talk is of little else. Hardly surprising when you discover that everyone at the bar has been affected personally.

Every member of the 20-strong charter company team (15 Thai, five Brits), whose 25 boats rock gently on pontoons just in front of us, have suffered bereavement, injury or financial loss.

The firm's Asia boss Kevin Quilty, 40, from Bexhill, East Sussex, his Thai wife Boom and their maid ran up to the first-floor balcony of their home at Khao Lak. Kevin watched as the building was knocked over and he and Boom grabbed part of the roof as they were swept inland for a mile. They survived. Their maid did not. Their £260 000 home was not insured for tsunami damage. But Kevin was philosophical about that. When I asked him if he will start all over again, he simply smiled and said: 'I would have died had Boom not woken me up. I was off-duty and asleep on the ground floor when she called me saying the tide had gone out too far'. He is just happy to be alive.

Charter skipper Paul Stamp, 38, who chucked in his job with local government in Sunderland to follow his dream job skippering in the sun is still traumatised by the event. He spent many days gathering up corpses and taking them to a make-shift morgue in Khao Lak.

'I'm pretty tough – I played rugby back home – but what I admire most is the strength of the Thais,' he said tears filling his eyes. He was offered three days off after the ordeal, but insisted instead on carrying on with the clean-up operation.

Superyacht skipper Alistair Purves, 38, from Whitby, North Yorks had watched a catamaran at Patong on the west coast of Phuket 'go almost vertical' in the wave. 'The skipper was wheelchair bound and thought he was going to die. Incredibly he survived,' he said.

Another yachtsman told me how the beach front at Patong had been mainly shops with plate glass windows: 'Imagine the wave laced with all those sheets of glass and you can imagine the sort of injuries which were sustained,' he said.

Our Jeanneau Sun Odyssey 45.2, *Carrioca,* nosed out through the mangroves of the Boat Lagoon – on the east side of Phuket – past the concrete piles marking the creek. Despite each one of them being topped with a sharp spike to prevent sea-eagles alighting upon them: guano was blotting out the red port-hand stripes.

Out on the horizon strange humped islands quivered in the heat haze and a fishing boat boiling up freshly caught whitebait sent clouds of steam into the brilliant blue sky.

'We often get customers call us up and say "There's a boat on fire, what shall we do ?"', said Simon James, 41, our skipper.

Office colleague Toby Hodges and I had signed up for the first charter since the wave.

Our first stop was Ko Nakha Noi, a small islet, just a few miles from Phuket, where we anchored for lunch. Toby and I swam ashore to a beach which appeared to be made from white flour. As we splashed up into the palms three Long Tom fish skittered away from our approach.

After lunch we proceeded north against a 1.5-knot current and dusk saw us approaching Ko Phanak island. This was one of the weirdly shaped humps we had seen in the distance. Up close its sheer sides were undermined by the sea and its underskirt of limestone stalactites looked like a herd of petrified stallions caught in their headlong plunge to the sea in a timeless frieze.

That night we anchored in Ko Hong, a roughly circle-shaped haven created from three different limestone island mountains. These mysterious islands are peculiar to Phang Nga Bay, a national park, and almost all of them, in silhouette, appear to be figures lying down including reclining buddhas, pregnant women and sleeping lantern-jawed males.

That night as we washed down barbeque-cooked steaks – imported from Australia – with chilled lager we lay back in the cockpit, still in our swimwear and gazed upon the starlit heavens.

In the morning a longtail boat ranged alongside. Her skipper, a fellow dressed in track suit bottoms and counterfeit Von Dutch designer shirt, slopped about in socked feet through six inches or so of bilge water to pluck a blue crab from beneath the aft thwart. Its luminous blue pincers clawed blindly at the fierce sun as it was offered to us. We declined and instead bought a bucket load of fresh tiger prawns for

300 baht (about £3.50). Happy with the deal the longtail skipper swung away: his engine unable to drown the squawking voice of a female squatting on the foredeck beneath a conical hat.

'She's saying he should have stood out for 500 baht,' said Simon, 'imagine going to work with your wife every day'.

Scaramanga's island with which he uses a giant rock-mounted satellite dish to reflect the rays of the sun to power up his weapon of mass destruction appeared over the horizon next. In reality Ko Phing Kan, better known as James Bond island since *The Man With The Golden Gun* was filmed here for the 1974 film, looks more like a giant sugar loaf.

Despite the film being over 30 years old, and described by some as the 'silliest' of the Bond movies, a pier has been built on the island to accommodate the tens of thousands of Bond fans who come here every year.

By now the oppressive sun – we were only 400-odd miles north of the equator – had begun to cook our pale winter skins and Toby and I fought back with sunblock, straw hats and sunglasses.

We sailed on to Ko Roi and launched the two kayaks *Carrioca* had lashed to her guardrails. Toby and I then paddled in Mohican-style towards a half-tide tunnel beside a sun-bleached beach. In the surf we ducked our heads and shot through the cave into the inner sanctum of Ko Roi. We were inside a 400-foot tall limestone 'cylinder'. It was like a ruined cathedral the ceiling of which had long ago collapsed. From its walls trees grew sideways from grotesque gargoyles of rock. Far away above us a blue disc of sky was flecked with circling sea-eagles. A snaking river led us on through this lost world in which it was easy to imagine prehistoric creatures may well be lurking. These places are called 'hongs', the Thai word for room.

We spent the night at anchor at Ko Chong Lot and were woken at dawn by what sounded like a chapter of clapped-out Hell's Angels setting off for a convention. The noise turned out to be a fleet of longtail boats off to chase prawn.

At the south-east end of Ko Chong Lot, we witnessed the first evidence of the tsunami legacy.

'That reef used to be just an evil rock, now it looks quite pretty,' said Simon, as he pointed to a longtail boat hauled up onto a sandy beach surrounding a black ridge of jagged rock. 'I suppose the wave just brought the sand up with it'.

We sailed south through the narrow gorge of Ko Man and onto Ko Hong Krabbi. Here the largest hong of them all is filled with strange limestone shapes of phalluses, intestinal parts, even a skeleton. Mangrove stems grew straight out of the sea floor like watercress and black crabs scampered over the razor-sharp rock skirts. Six wrecked longtail boats and one motor cruiser lay 100 yards from the water up in among the palms.

That afternoon we pressed on to the anchorage at Railay Bay, passing en route two Thai warships anchored off a golden roofed palace: one of the summer residences of King Bhumibol, whose grandson Bhumi, 21, was killed while on a jet ski off the mainland resort of Khao Lak when the tsunami struck.

At Railay Beach were the shattered remains of a 21 ft yacht, and we were told by one resident that a beachfront house had provided some light relief to the tsunami's grim reaping: 'For days the owner was able to hook fish swimming around on the ground floor inside the threshold of her home,' he said.

Our next destination was Laem Ko Kwang on the island of Ko Lanta Ya. Here the north end of the bay was showing marked tsunami damage. Concrete pylons carrying overhead voltage had been snapped off like pencils: but two engineers had their pickup parked on the beach, doors open so that as they worked methodically through the collapsed spans they could enjoy the vehicle's CD player. Here was a whole holiday complex of bungalows which had been damaged: a wall gone here, a roof partly torn off there, half-empty muddy swimming pools, and several scores of mattresses stacked like cards awaiting disposal. As I peered into the once intimate interiors I became aware of the tsunami's random character: looking into a bungalow with blown out walls and semi-collapsed roof I was suddenly staring at myself in a full length, uncracked mirror. A sole longtail boat up in the tree line had already been stripped of its engine. I noticed an army of large red ants had mobilised and were crawling up its stern line, and marching along the starboard gunnel as they surveyed their unexpected windfall of building materials.

'It's like a nuclear fallout zone,' said Toby, 'eerie'.

We anchored off Monkey Beach on the north-west side of Phi Phi Don island the following night. Here only the large chunks of coral head thrown high up above the tideline told of the great forces which had been unleashed. Otherwise all was perfect: a white beach fringed by monkey-chattering jungle. That night the pulse of fishing boat engines rolled in across the perfect sea as a fleet of squid-fishing boats trained their brilliant lights into the deep to lure out their myopic prize.

Another 'crop' is regularly gathered around these islands: the regurgitated saliva of swifts with which they make nests. Such organic matter is used in the much sought after bird's nest soup – American dealers pay £1 500 a kilo – and many of the nest harvesters fall to their deaths each year from rickety bamboo scaffolds, several of which we spotted clinging to sheer rock face 400 feet up.

The next morning we visited the staggeringly beautiful Maya Bay on nearby Phi Phi Le: here it was that film star Leonardo di Caprio strode across the sand for the 1998 film *The Beach*. Toby and I went snorkelling and hand-fed bananas and slices of bread to shoals of those fish which had escaped the attentions of trawlers and longtail nets.

Our final destination was the by now notorious Ton Sai Bay at Phi Phi Don island – one of the worst hit areas on the yachting circuit. Here 1 500 people died and 4 000 were injured. Its problem was simply geographical: a low beach isthmus joins two mountainous sections of island. It was on this low lying land that the main resort was located. It received a double-whammy as the tsunami roared across sweeping the village both from the north and the south: like the Biblical Red Sea closing over the Egyptians.

We took the inflatable onto the beach and strode through the remains of the town which looked like a mini-Stalingrad post 1942, except that sheer volume of water is more effective than armour-piercing shells or artillery. One vast bungalow complex – to the west of the isthmus – had simply disappeared, the old part of the town was now three huge piles of rubble, what was left standing was in a state of semi-collapse.

Thai electricians sat in the shade splicing a thousand wires together. Australian, British and German dive shop workers were wheel-barrowing rubble to the three large piles and two JCBs were filling a lighter with detritus. Massive bonfires were blazing: fuelled with unsalveagable and contaminated rubbish: clothing, handbags and the ubiquitous trainer.

One told us: 'Stock is the problem: the Thais won't use anything that is left, they say it is full of bad spirits'. I found a torn photograph blowing along the rubbish-strewn street. It depicted six youngsters enjoying themselves in a bar. I wondered where they were now.

A sign pinned on a door frame read: 'Don't be a disaster tourist, spend some money here now'.

Back at the Watermark Bar the mood had changed. The talk was still of the tsunami but now there was laughter, especially at the story of the yachtsman whose anchor had fouled an ATM machine in Phi Phi Don.

Throughout Thailand red ribbons and garlands are being draped afresh around newly launched boats. Now they just need passengers.

Bibliography: *Yachting Monthly*, April 2005, vol. 1, 184, Dick Durham.

THE MYSTERIOUS VOYAGE OF THE *MARY CELESTE*

Many theories have been put forward about what happened to the crew of the *Mary Celeste*, you may have your own once you've read the story

On the afternoon of 5 December 1872, the brig *Dei Gratia*, on passage from New York to Gibraltar spotted a sail ahead and despite the light northerly wind she slowly gained on her. Both ships were half-way between the Azores and the Portuguese coast.

As the *Dei Gratia* steered closer her skipper, Captain Morehouse, recognised the vessel as the 98 ft brigantine *Mary Celeste*. Just a month before she had been alongside a wharf in New York, loading barrels of commercial alcohol for Genoa, Italy. The *Dei Gratia*, had been loading nearby.

Morehouse and the *Mary Celeste's* captain Benjamin Briggs were old friends, and had dined together in New York the evening before Briggs sailed.

Now the puzzled captain looked at his old pal's ship swinging on and off course: one minute luffing up into the wind and the next falling off a point or two and with her jib and foretopmast-staysail aback. Morehouse signalled her but received no reply. Then through his telescope he saw there was no one at the wheel. Nor was anyone visible on deck, yet Briggs had a crew of seven, plus his wife and their two-year-old daughter when they sailed.

Neither an 'urgent' signal-hoist nor hailing the ship produced a response so Morehouse shortened sail, lowered a boat, and with his first mate, Oliver Deveau, went to investigate.

As they drew alongside they noticed the davit falls which should have been holding the *Mary Celeste's* small boat, were empty and trailing in the water.

The deck was deserted and in the main cabin was a sewing-machine on the table, and beside it a reel of cotton, a thimble and a small oil-can, objects which would have been flung to the deck had the ship rolled. There were also the remains of a meal, and an unfinished letter by Richardson, the mate.

The bunks had been neatly made up, and on one a pillow carried the impression of a child's head. Petty cash and trinkets, including a gold locket, were left undisturbed and Briggs' clothes were neatly stowed in drawers and his wife's trunks contained clothing including the baby girl's full outfit.

But then they discovered the galley store-room drawers, normally containing tins of preserved meat, had been emptied. The ship's papers, her chronometer and her sextant were also missing.

In the fo'c'sle seamen's chests were full and washing was hanging up to dry. Various small amounts of money and intimate personal affects, were lying untouched.

Mary Celeste's bilges were dry, and her cargo properly stowed and unbroached.

The ship's log contained only seven entries, the last of them noted 11 days before when she was 100 miles west of the island of Santa Maria in the Azores. The 'rough slate' contained one more entry placing the *Mary Celeste* six miles north-north-east of Santa Maria a day later.

One of the hatchway covers had been removed. It lay, upside-down, which from that day on joined the lexicon of seaman's superstitions: it would now be considered unlucky to lay a hatch board the wrong way up. A cutlass, exhibiting what were thought to be traces of blood, was also discovered. One of the wooden upper-deck rails displayed a gash which might have been made by an axe, and close by, on the deck, were two or three spots, apparently of blood.

Morehouse ordered his mate to sail the *Mary Celeste* in convoy with the *Dei Gratia* to Gibraltar and both ships eventually arrived safely. Investigations were made by the Marshal of the Vice-Admiralty Court, four naval post-captains, and a colonel of the Royal Engineers. A local doctor determined that the smears on the cutlass were rust, not blood.

A survey found either side of the bows, a couple of feet or so above the waterline, a groove about an inch wide, and seven feet long, apparently recently made with a sharp instrument.

On 25 March 1873, the Vice Admiralty Court at Gibraltar gave judgement. It awarded £1 700 to the *Dei Gratia* for salvage.

With an apprehensive fresh crew the *Mary Celeste* was sailed to Genoa, where her cargo was discharged.

Back in the USA she was considered a 'voodoo ship' and sailors tried to avoid her. She made her last voyage at the end of 1884, from Boston for Haiti with a mixed cargo. On 3 January 1885, she ran on to Roshell's Reef, off the Haitian coast, and became a total loss. Investigations found her owners had induced the skipper to run her ashore to enable the insurance to be claimed. He died before the case reached adjudication. The mate died three months later, one of the shippers committed suicide, all of the firms who had a hand in the fraud went bankrupt, and the very ship which rescued the *Mary Celeste's* crew was wrecked, with loss of life, on her next voyage.

Many theories of the *Mary Celeste's* abandonment have been mooted and dismissed, the first being that of mutiny by the crew. In this scenario the crew breach barrels, imbibe virtually undrinkable crude alcohol, murder the captain, his wife and baby and then scour two marks on the bow giving the ship the appearance of running aground.

But no mutineers were ever picked up.

Another is that it was the result of a conspiracy between Briggs and Morehouse. But Briggs, was part-owner of the ship, and would have been personally liable for his share of the salvage costs. And both he and Morehouse were men of excellent character and reputation.

Another is that an outbreak of plague killed some of the crew and drove the remainder to abandon the ship. But the chances of escaping such contagion would be much slimmer in the boat than on board the ship.

Yet another is that *Mary Celeste* was blown off course towards the African coast. As she lay becalmed near the shore, a party of pirates set out to board her, and the crew used their only chance of escape by abandoning ship. The raiders then sank the boat and all in it. But on making for the deserted ship, they found her sails filled by a rising breeze, and were run down and sunk while attempting to board her over the bows – hence the marks found at Gibraltar.

But exhaustive inquiries made at the time along the African coast threw nothing up.

Another expert suggested that on 27 November 1872, when the *Mary Celeste* was a few miles off Santa Maria, a smell of gas, or rumbling noises, indicated that the cargo was on the point of exploding. Briggs ordered one of the hatches to be uncovered, to let the gas disperse. As this was being done a slight explosion occurred, overturning the hatch. Fearing that the ship might blow up at any moment, he gave orders to abandon her. The boat may have been capsized when getting clear or, wrecked when attempting to land.

It is unlikely now that anyone will ever know what actually happened to the *Mary Celeste*.

THE MYSTERIOUS VOYAGE OF JOHN FRANKLIN

The quest to find the North-West Passage led to death and disaster for John Franklin's expedition. But the gruesome details of his crew's last days were only revealed years later

In April 1852 the English brig *Renovation*, on passage from Limerick to Quebec, was skirting a large ice-floe off the Newfoundland Banks. At 6 am the ship's mate, Robert Simpson, who was on watch, called for his telescope. He focused the glass on the most surreal sight he had ever seen in all his years at sea. Some three miles off, two three-masted ships, close together, one heeled over the other upright, sat on top of a gigantic iceberg. Was Simpson looking at the *Erebus* and *Terror*, the Royal Naval sailing ships taken by Sir John Franklin deep into the Arctic ice six years before in 1845 while trying to find the

North-West Passage? Four years before Simpson's encounter in 1848 when all 129 men and the two ships had disappeared without trace, Victorian society was deeply shocked and search parties were sent out.

The Franklin Expedition set sail from Greenhithe, England, on the morning of 19 May 1845, and sailed north to Aberdeen for supplies. From Scotland, the ships sailed to Greenland with HMS *Rattler* and a transport ship, *Barretto Junior*.

Franklin's orders were to try and find a channel through unexplored polar seas south-west from Cape Walker in northern Canada. If this failed then he was to try and forge a passage through the Wellington Channel. One of these passages, it was hoped, would lead to the Bering Strait and then a route, north around the Americas, would have been established. His ships had seen tough service in the Antarctic under another polar explorer Sir James Ross. They were sea kindly and very strong having originally been built as bomb ketches with planking designed to withstand the recoil of heavy mortars fired skywards from their decks. For their polar work the planking and the framing had been doubled.

Franklin who sailed aboard the *Erebus* was, at 59, considered too old for such a gruelling voyage, but he was full of enthusiasm and the discovery of the North-West Passage would have been the crowning moment of a very successful naval career.

The expedition was seen on 26 July 1845, when Captain Dannett of the whaler *Prince of Wales* encountered *Terror* and *Erebus* moored to an iceberg in Melville Bay, Greenland. He was told by the explorers that they were waiting for the ice to break up before crossing into Lancaster Sound.

Later that month the crew of another whaler, *Enterprise*, encountered the explorers. They were still waiting to make their start on the passage but were in good health and high spirits.

That was the last time they were seen alive by Europeans.

No news came back to the world's greatest imperial power, the British Empire, that year or the next, and by the time the days were getting shorter in the northern hemisphere in the autumn of 1847 it was feared something had gone very wrong.

It was known that the expedition had stores enough to carry them through until June 1848, but still the silence boded ill. Calls for a sledging party to be sent out overland from Hudson Bay were ignored but were subsequently proved to have been a sound plan.

In the spring of 1848 the Admiralty sent Sir James Ross in the ships *Enterprise* and *Investigator* to find the lost expedition. His mission failed.

Further attempted rescues were made by both British and American naval parties and a ship was sent by Franklin's wife but all to no avail. Ironically, the North-West Passage was successfully completed by the *Investigator*, under Commander Robert McClure, during a second bid to find Franklin, this time coming in from the Pacific end.

At the end of 1851 on Beechey Island near the Wellington Channel three graves, some abandoned huts and a pile of empty meat tins were found: evidence that Franklin had wintered there.

Next, a bizarre incident occurred when a balloon carrying a message arrived in a garden near Wootton Lodge, near Gloucester. It read: '*Erebus*. 112 degrees West longitude, 70 degrees North latitude. September 3rd, 1851. Blocked in'.

It turned out to be a hoax: neither of Franklin's ships had been supplied with balloons.

Then in the spring of 1852 Robert Simpson, the mate of the *Renovation*, spotted the two ships on an ice-floe. No sign of any human life could be seen through the telescope which was passed around the whole crew. The master of the *Renovation* was in his sick bed and would not allow closer investigation. The mystery ships were later seen by the crew of another vessel, the German brig *Doctor Kneip*.

The crews of both ships should have taken a detour to investigate as the Admiralty had offered £20 000 to anyone rendering assistance to Franklin's expedition.

In the spring of 1852 the last official search was sent out by the Admiralty commanded by Sir Edward Belcher who had no Arctic experience. After two years with five ships in the Wellington Channel he returned with just one – a performance for which he was court-martialled.

In 1854 at last some news about Franklin's fate came from Dr John Rae who worked for the Hudson's Bay Company and 'went native' on hunting expeditions for months on end. During one of these he met a group of Eskimos in Pelly Bay. They told him that six years earlier they had come across a party of 40 thin white men who were dragging a boat south over the ice near the west side of King William Island. He was told both the ships they had been sailing on had become icebound. The men had tried to reach safety on foot but had succumbed to cold and some had resorted to cannibalism, news which led to widespread revulsion in Victorian society. Later the same year, these Eskimos found 30 dead bodies on the north shore of the Canadian mainland and five more on a nearby island. Rae bought some relics from the Eskimos which included watches, parts of telescopes, compasses, firearms, silver spoons and forks, and a silver plate with Franklin's name engraved on it.

In the light of this revelation the Admiralty declined to invest any more cash into the Franklin mystery: it was clear they were all dead and no more men's lives should be risked in trying to find further evidence. But Lady Franklin thought otherwise. She clung to the hope that some of the men, unable to get back to the mainland might be living with the Eskimos. She raised enough money to equip a steam yacht the *Fox* commanded by Francis McClintock. They sailed in 1857 and spent eight months beset in pack ice in Melville Bay. But he refused to give up. By 1859 two parties from the *Fox* started searching King William Island. They found more relics, several unburied skeletons, discarded clothing and equipment, and then a sinister discovery: two headless skeletons with guns which had fired a single shot in an abandoned ship's boat mounted on a sledge. And finally they discovered a cairn at Victory Point in which a metal container held two messages on rust-streaked note paper. One was from James Fitzjames, captain of *Erebus*, in which he recorded that *Erebus* and *Terror* were deserted on 22 April 1848 having been beset in ice since 12 September 1846. The note also recorded the death of Franklin on 11 June 1847. The exact location of his grave is unknown.

In the mid-1980s, Owen Beattie, a University of Alberta professor of anthropology, concluded Franklin and his men had most likely died of pneumonia and perhaps tuberculosis. Toxicological reports indicated that lead poisoning from tinned food was also a possible factor. Later in 1997 blade cut marks on the bones of some of the crew found on King William Island suggested that some may have resorted to cannibalism.

A combination of scurvy, poisoned food, botulism and starvation had killed everyone in the Franklin party.

In October 2009 fragments of sheet metal and copper were recovered from 19th century Inuit hunting sites were believed to have come from the protective sheathing of the *Terror*'s hull.

THE RAFT OF THE *MEDUSA*

The subject of a world-famous painting by Gericault, the shipwreck of the *Medusa*, became a national scandal in France when it was revealed that her officers and crew were involved in desertion, drunkenness, murder and cannibalism

French artist Théodore Géricault's painting, *Raft of the Medusa*, confronts the visitor to the Louvre, Paris, with epic proportions: it's 16 ft high by a massive 23 ft in width. The Romantic painter knew it would take a broad canvas to portray what was at the time a national scandal. But though Géricault visited hospitals and morgues to study the dying and the dead and even let body parts decay in his studio, no picture could ever tell the horrific story of the suffering which befell those aboard the 44-gun French frigate *Medusa*.

In June 1816, the *Medusa* set sail from Rochefort, halfway down France's Biscay coastline, with three other ships bound for the Senegalese port of Saint-Louis, which had been given to the French by the British as a show of good faith to the reinstated French king, Louis XVIII, following the downfall of Napoleon Bonaparte. The ship held nearly 400 people, including women and children and the new French governor of Senegal, Colonel Julien Schmaltz, travelling with his wife and three daughters and his 252 soldiers from African colonies under French officers and 160 crew members. The captain was Hugues Deroys, Vicomte de Chaumareys, 53, who had not been to sea in 25 years and had never commanded a ship before, but who was a friend of Louis XVIII.

After narrowly averting an early grounding in the shoals of his home waters Chaumareys angered his crew, who later were even further alarmed at the dismissive treatment shown by their haughty captain after a cabin boy fell overboard. De Chaumareys was reluctant to slow the ship down to rescue the lad, but after a dangerous delay allowed a rescue boat to be lowered. The boat was manned by crew who were afraid to row too far from the ship in case they became the next victims of their captain's haste to be on his way. Without any serious attempt at a search they returned to the ship and reported that the boy had been drowned.

De Chaumareys' wavering course added an unnecessary 100 miles to an arrival at Madeira where they took on stores, and after a further call for provisions at Tenerife the captain relied on a smooth-talking philanthropist, M. Richefort, for the ship's navigation. Richefort had flattered de Chaumareys and professed local knowledge of the Arguin Reef which stuck out 100 miles from the African coast about 300 miles north of Senegal. Under Richefort's sailing directions the *Medusa* sailed straight onto the sandy reef at almost high water. Suggestions were made to lighten the ship by dumping the cannons overboard but de Chaumareys wouldn't hear of it for fear of angering his royal sponsors back in France.

The *Medusa* had sailed onto the reef in calm weather, but the following night a breeze got up. Bumping over the sand, the frigate's rudder was unshipped and, swinging freely on its steering chains, damaged some of the stern planking causing the vessel to start leaking.

As the wind increased, the ship pounded more heavily and broke her back. They were 60 miles from the African coast: 400 souls with six lifeboats capable of carrying 250.

Rumours that de Chaumareys and Governor Schmaltz were planning to make a getaway in one of the boats ran round the ship, causing many of the soldiers to rush at their officers. They were beaten back down below under sword and rifle fire. And then Schmaltz announced his plan: that a raft would be built to hold the troops and that this raft would be towed to safety by the lifeboats – in which would be the passengers and crew.

The raft, built of fallen spars and ship's planking and lashed together with warps was 66 ft long and 22 ft wide. Eventually, everyone was forced to abandon ship. The wealthy and well-connected were given space on the lifeboats while the rest, 149 people, were forced onto the makeshift raft.

Now the overladen lifeboats found it difficult to make steerage way towing the cumbersome raft and one after the other found reason not to be attached to it. Those on the raft heard a chilling cry from the barge – the vessel carrying both the captain and the governor – 'Let us abandon them' and the tow rope was cut.

The lifeboats, unhampered by the raft now made a relatively easy passage to shore. The occupants made their way overland or by rescue ship to St Louis and were hailed as heroes until news of the raft unfolded.

A naturalist, Correard and a surgeon Savigny wrote up a detailed account of the raft's two-week nightmare. The pair rigged up a mast and managed to set a sail, but steering the craft was difficult and the sail could only be set when the wind blew onshore, otherwise they would have been blown further out to sea. Many of the castaways took solace in wine rations from barrels included in the raft's provisions. But when they were refused extra draughts they became aggressive and speculated on what they would do to those who had left them behind.

Savigny recalled: 'It was now that we had need of all our courage, which, however, forsook us more than once. We really believed we were sacrificed, and with one accord we cried that this desertion was premeditated. We all swore to revenge ourselves if we had the good fortune to reach the shore, and there is no doubt that if we could have overtaken the next day those who had fled in the boats, an obstinate combat would have taken place between us and them'.

After a night-time gale 20 men were missing: some had been swept overboard, others had been crushed to death, having fallen between the grinding spars of the raft itself. As the days went on hunger and thirst drove some men to jump overboard.

Further heavy weather terrified the landsmen among the castaways who thought their last moments had come and decided that oblivion would be best confronted in drink. They overruled the officers, and bored a hole in a wine cask. Savigny's story continues: 'The fumes of the wine disordered their brains already affected by the presence of danger and want of food. Thus inflamed, these men, become deaf to the voice of reason, desired to implicate in one common destruction their companions in misfortune'.

One of the drunks started chopping at the raft's vital cords with an axe and this started an onboard battle between mutineers and the rest. In the ensuing fight 60 men died. Savigny added:

> 'Those whom death had spared fell upon the dead bodies with which the raft was covered and cut off pieces; of which some was instantly devoured. Seeing that this horrid nourishment had given strength to those who had made use of it, it was proposed to dry it, in order to render it a little less disgusting. Those who had the firmness enough to abstain from it took a larger quantity of wine.
>
> We tried to eat swordbelts and cartouche-boxes, and succeeded in swallowing some little morsels. Some ate linen, others pieces of leather from the hats, on which there was a little grease, or rather dirt. A sailor attempted to eat excrement, but he could not succeed.

A shoal of 200 flying fish was also mixed with human flesh, which up until now had been refused by officers. They were now ready to eat their colleagues because the fish had 'rendered it less disgusting'.

Following the 'feast' a second mutiny took place at the end of which only 30 of the original 147 occupants were left on the raft. Now that rations were so scarce even the civilised members of the castaways turned bestial and the fittest among them – including Correard and Savigny – threw the weak and dying into the sea.

After 17 days just 15 survivors were picked up by the rescue brig *Argus* which had sailed from St Louis to find them. Five of those died shortly after their deliverance. Once Correard and Savigny's account was published both de Chaumareys and Schmaltz were recalled to France in disgrace. De Chaumareys was court-martialled, then acquitted because the French feared ridicule from the British for putting such an incompetent officer in charge in the first place.

THE RIDDLE OF ERSKINE CHILDERS

The man who wrote one of the most famous sailing novels of all time was a complex romantic who ended his life in front of a firing squad

In July 1914 two yachts were rafted up alongside a German tug anchored near the Ruytingen Light Vessel off the coast of Belgium. One of them was a fine looking gaff-rigged ketch, just nine years old. She was *Asgard* a 50 ft Colin Archer, a wedding present to yachtsman, author and politician Erskine Childers from his father-in-law. She was loading 900 second-hand Mauser rifles and 29 000 rounds of ammunition. The second yacht was *Kelpie*, a fine 60-footer owned by Irish yachtsman Conor O'Brien.

Just a couple of weeks before the transhipment taking place in the English Channel, Kaiser Wilhelm II of Germany was aboard his own yacht *Meteor V* at the prestigious Elbe Regatta, behind the sands of the Frisian Islands, when he received news of the assassination in Serbia of heir to the throne of the Austro-Hungarian empire, Franz Ferdinand.

By the time *Asgard's* accommodation had been ripped out and the wrappings of the rifles removed so as to fill the yacht with as much weaponry as possible, the great European empires were already mobilising down the road to World War I .

The wind was blowing from the south-west and Childers faced a long beat down Channel in his overladen yacht, now down on her marks and with the rifles stacked within two feet of the deck beams. More rifles were stacked in the yacht's doghouse forming lumpy 'bunks' for the off watch crew. When her stability was in question Childers dumped 4 000 rounds of ammunition overboard.

Off Plymouth the man who had resigned his membership of the Liberal Party to devote his life to Irish Home Rule got a shock when he thought he had come under fire from British warships, but it turned out they were on a pre-war exercise live-firing at a floating target.

Childers' cargo was unloaded at Howth near Dublin, on 26 July. O'Brien's rifles were landed a week later. The weapons were for the Irish Republicans: Childers had become alarmed at the fact that the Ulster Volunteer Force had been arming themselves and he felt the South would be defenceless against them.

But although Childers supported Irish independence he was no enemy of England. Later the same year he joined the Royal Naval Volunteer Force and later the Royal Naval Air Service – receiving the D.S.C. for leading the first naval air raid on Cuxhaven, another port behind the shoals he had made famous with his novel *The Riddle of the Sands*, published 11 years earlier in 1903.

This book about two men in the sailing boat, *Dulcibella*, who, while cruising around the Dutch and German Frisian Islands, stumble upon a plan for invasion of England by Germany, has become an all time classic of small-boat sailing and a Hollywood film.

Winston Churchill, when First Lord of the Admiralty, said that the novel was instrumental in persuading public opinion to back funding for naval bases at Invergordon, Rosyth and Scapa Flow against such a German threat.

Childers became secretary-general of the Irish delegation that negotiated the Anglo-Irish Treaty with the British government, but became opposed to the setting up of the Irish Free State and therefore made enemies among those Irish who backed it believing it was better than nothing.

Now a notorious figure he was arrested at his home in Glendalough, County Wicklow and tried by a military court for possessing a firearm in violation of the Emergency Powers Resolution.

He was sentenced to death by firing squad in November 1922 and famously told his executioners: 'Take a step forward, lads. It will be easier that way'.

The Ruytingen Light Vessel has now gone, but a buoy still twists and turns in the strong tides of the Dover Strait marking the spot where Childers' yachting abilities crossed tack with his political ideology.

PART SEVEN

Rescue

FROZEN TO THE RIGGING

The worst blizzard to hit the south coast of Britain in 200 years wrecked many ships. One of them was the smart square-rigger *Bay of Panama*, the bones of which can be seen to this day

One morning in March 1891 a lone shepherd was battling through 20 foot snowdrifts covering the fields which teeter over the entrance to the Helford River in Cornwall. He was endeavouring to find some of his lost flock after the worst blizzard to hit England for 200 years. He soon discovered that the missing sheep and even some cows had frozen to death in the Arctic conditions and was about to retrace his Yeti-like steps back to the warmth of his cottage when to his astonishment he saw the skeletal masts of a giant sailing ship sticking up from the rocks below Nare Point. Pushing through the deep snow at the cliff edge for a better look he was aghast at the sight of a 90 m (270 ft) four-masted, full rigged ship beached and rolling in the swell with her spars snapped off like matchsticks and her sails just so many rags strewn over the side. To his horror he counted nine figures hanging in the rigging of the aft mast.

The good shepherd was looking down on the wreck of the *Bay of Panama*, 112 days out from Calcutta bound for Dundee with 17 000 bales of jute.

She was built in 1883 by Messrs Harland and Wolff, of Belfast, a vessel of 2 282 gross registered tons, belonging to Bullock's Bay Line, of London. She had already made several fast passages from Calcutta in the jute trade and many sailors regarded her as one of the best looking ships ever launched.

Her master, David Wright, was accompanied by his wife, and had as crew two mates, five apprentices, and 22 fo'c'sle hands of all nationalities, giving the *Bay of Panama* a total complement of 31 hands.

The winter of 1890–91 had been exceptionally hard with weeks of severe frost. The UK was relieved to feel temperatures rise during February, and during the first few days of March it was even shirt-sleeve weather. But winter came back with a vengeance on 8 March just as the *Bay of Panama* came onto soundings in the English Channel.

Captain Wright steered a course to make his landfall off the Lizard, but as the visibility shut in he saw no sign of the famed headland and by noon the following day the *Bay of Panama* was hard-pressed clawing into an easterly gale, laced with heavy snow and punching a rising sea. As the wind increased the crew went aloft and reduced her sail to the four lower-topsails, after which Captain Wright put her helm up and hove-to on the starboard tack. Soon the mizzen and jigger lower-topsails were stowed as well, as Captain Wright deliberately took speed off her hoping the weather would clear before he neared land. He avoided putting the ship on the other tack and heading off clear of the land, for fear of running into other vessels in the busy Channel waters.

As the day wore on the blizzard grew in intensity and by nightfall reached hurricane force carrying away the two remaining topsails. The freezing conditions soon turned the masts, yards, rigging, footropes and ratlines, into a giant ice sculpture and going aloft became a risky business. The crew who were taking soundings with the leadline found their hands had turned to frozen claws and the codline with the weight on the end slipped through their rigid fingers and disappeared over the side. Visibility was now down to 600 feet, and as Captain Wright feared he must be close to land, he tried to bring the ship round onto the other tack and sail her away from terra firma.

But the *Bay of Panama* was now under bare poles and would not respond to her helm. Two staysails were hoisted to try and wear her round but they quickly blew out.

Although she was still heading northwards to the unseen rocks of the Lizard, Captain Wright sent the off-duty watch below for some rest. There was, after all, little that anyone could do. But Captain Wright himself remained at his station on the poop deck staring ahead into the blizzard trying to piece together a shape out of the formless flurries. This was interspersed with quick visits to study the chart, or to the cabin below to try and reassure his anxious wife.

In the early hours of Tuesday, 10 March, the watch became aware that the ship was no longer heaving up and down through the long seas, but jumping and jolting through a confused sea surface which Captain Wright knew meant only one thing: shoal water.

The captain ordered distress rockets to be prepared for firing, but almost immediately afterwards the *Bay of Panama* shivered as her keel juddered on the bottom. Next a huge breaking wave lifted her clear before she slid, surreally stern-first, down its back and hit the ground again with such violence that this time men were knocked flat. The next huge comber roared out of the darkness and exploded aboard, swamping the great steel ship half-way up her masts as she rolled into it.

The wave left the ship a complete wreck. As it drained away it dragged with it the matchwood it had made of the ship's wheel, wheelbox, skylight, charthouse and poop bulkhead. Water gushed out of the saloon and deckhouse which were stripped out. The deluge also swept away Captain Wright, his wife, the second mate, four of the five apprentices, the carpenter, boatswain, sailmaker, cook and steward, to their deaths in the icy breakers. The mate, who had been washed off the poop on to the main deck, and jammed beneath the main fife-rail, staggered to the jigger rigging, and yelled at his shipmates to follow him aloft.

By now the *Bay of Panama's* steel hull was splitting apart as she pounded on the granite ledge, with her starboard bulwarks, wrenched off and lying broadside to the seas. All her boats were reduced to splinters or torn from their davit hooks in the first deluge of water; and the mizzen mast was broken off. The watch below were washed from their bunks in the fo'c'sle when the ship grounded. But they decided to remain in their quarters, sheltering as best they could from the freezing temperatures and seas on deck.

With the epic image of the stricken ship seared in his mind, the shepherd made his way back to the village of St Keverne to raise the alarm. But St Keverne was cut off from the outside world and did not possess any life-saving apparatus. And so, a young farmer, Joseph James, volunteered to take a pony and get a message to Helston, 10 miles away, to telegraph Falmouth. After a hellish, snow-bound journey to Helston he discovered that all the telegraph wires were down. And so he determined to walk to Falmouth, a further 12 miles. Before he had got halfway the messenger was so tired and cold he had to crawl through the deepening snow, on his hands and knees. That night overcome with exhaustion he took shelter in a roadside cottage. As soon as dawn broke he continued and arrived in Falmouth mid-morning.

When a salvage tug towing the lifeboat, arrived at the wreck they found she had been driven too far inshore to be reached. But in the meantime the rocket apparatus had been dragged overland, through the deep drifts, and 16 survivors were brought ashore in the breeches buoy. Six of the crew, including the mate, who had lashed themselves to the rigging were found frozen to death.

Today, more than 120 years on, at certain stages of the tide, ramblers can still make out the outline of a ship below the cliffs at Nare Point.

GOOD SAMARITAN OF THE SOUTHERN OCEAN

To rescue a shipwrecked sailor at sea is one thing. To accomplish it as a solo sailor in the Southern Ocean by beating upwind against a storm is another and perhaps one only Pete Goss could achieve

It's the toughest race in the world and it's around the world. The Vendée Globe, invented by a Frenchman, starts in the Biscay port of Les Sables D'Olonne and those who cross the finish line there some three months later will have sailed 25 000 miles or so, non-stop alone. They will have passed the great and feared corners of the world including the Cape of Good Hope and Cape Horn, survived hurricane-force winds, dodged ice-floes, shivered through sub-zero temperatures, and all on an average of five hours' sleep a day.

But at least they will be following a well-known pattern of prevailing winds. Though this cannot be relied upon 100 per cent, the boats should, in theory, be going downwind. In the terrible Southern Ocean the great westerlies roll round the bottom of the world with nothing to stop them building up 50-foot waves. The boats these heroes sail, should be on a non-stop sleigh ride with speeds of up to 30 knots at times.

If you careered along at that pace in Britain's metropolis you'd be breaking the speed limit.

So now imagine if you are on your boat in the Southern Ocean with a hurricane behind you hanging on for dear life and willing Cape Horn to be done with when the telephone rings – in this case a satcom unit – and someone asks you to TURN ROUND.

That's what happened to former Royal Marine Commando Pete Goss on Christmas Day 1996 when a distress call was passed on to his automatic receiver from the Marine Rescue Control Centre in Australia. They were alerting Goss to the fact that a fellow competitor in the race, Frenchman Raphael Dinelli was in trouble and needed help. When Goss checked the position he discovered to his horror that Dinelli's boat was 160 miles away up wind.

It was just as well for Dinelli that Goss *was* a former Royal Marine Commando, for without a second's hesitation, he gybed the boat round. Now in 60 knots of hell he started under storm jib to make an incredible 8 knots of speed although only at 80 degrees to the blast. But Goss knew the wind had to ease eventually.

That was not much consolation to his wife Tracey. Goss faxed her to let her know what was happening before she heard it through the press. In his fax he wrote something he'd never written before: 'Don't worry', which, of course, had the opposite effect.

Goss was forced to strap himself into his bunk as his Open 60 *Aqua Quorum* was being knocked down every 30 minutes in the maelstrom. He had taken some bruising from stores flying around and a can of oil was causing his live generator to spark and splutter: all he needed now was a fire on board to deal with as well.

Goss's incredible mix of physical toughness and intellect tracked down the Frenchman after two days. His boat *Algimouss* had sunk and he was in a life-raft. Goss had worked so well to get upwind of Dinelli that he had overshot him by seven miles and was zig-zagging back down his rhumb line to find him. Goss was by now being given positions by an overflying Royal Australian Air Force plane and as they flew over Dinelli they flashed some wing lights.

'I took the best bearing of my life,' Goss wryly noted later on.

He successfully picked up the half-frozen Frenchman, rubbed him down with a towel, dressed him in a set of spare thermals and packed him into his sleeping bag. With medication and a slowly administered routine of physiotherapy, Goss nursed him back to life. It took five days to get him walking again.

Goss dropped Dinelli in Hobart and went back to the race. He now had no hope of winning it, but that mattered little to the outside world who were impressed and moved by his selfless courage. So too was President Chirac of France who awarded Goss the Legion d'Honneur for saving one of his citizens.

MYSTERY FIRE AT SEA

Eric Hiscock is a legend among the Blue Water cruising fraternity, for both his voyages and the books he wrote about them. But his strangest encounter was much nearer to home

The boat on which amateur sailor, and three times circumnavigator Eric Hiscock died in 1986 was called *Wanderer V.* It says everything about the small, albino-like, bespectacled ocean vagabond. For in that boat and the four other *Wanderers* which came before her, he had sailed – with his wife Susan as crew – across oceans, up creeks and through canals. In 50 years of sailing he wrote 12 books and was awarded with the top gongs of prestigious yacht clubs. But he was always candid: never believing in his own publicity.

Probably the strangest encounter at sea he ever had was not in some far flung location most yachtsmen just dream about, but in the English Channel at night while sailing solo from Falmouth back to his home port Yarmouth in the Solent aboard his second *Wanderer*, a 24 ft gaff cutter *Wanderer II*.

Rolling along with a fair wind from the west, *Wanderer II* was making 5.5 knots when at 2 am on the first night out Hiscock spotted a red glow off the starboard bow out in the Channel.

At first Hiscock thought it was the bleary lights of a trawler, but as its bearing was changing fast he knew it was near and therefore altered course to determine what it was. He discovered a 40 ft white motor-cruiser with smoke pouring from her and the deck house ablaze. With his poor eyesight and a freshening breeze it was a serious feat of seamanship for Hiscock to get *Wanderer II* close enough to the blazing hull. First of all he hove-to and dropped the topsail then beat back to the stricken boat. His biggest fear was of imminent explosion – especially if the craft was petrol driven. He sailed close to and found two crew crouching in the stern sheets. He yelled that he would come back, make a close run alongside and that when he shouted they should jump. He lowered the peak of his gaff mainsail, and hauled his boom in tight to take way off the boat. As he approached the motor-boat he let his jib and staysail sheets fly and sent up a flare. But his first run in was too cautious: for fear of entangling his rigging with the burning boat *Wanderer II* was too far for the crew to jump. But then a steep sea threw *Wanderer II* very close and Hiscock yelled: 'Jump'.

The two crew landed successfully on his foredeck just as *Wanderer's* rigging did indeed foul the wreck, but fortunately only her flagstaff snapped off.

A man and a woman came crawling aft and Hiscock asked if there was anyone else on board.

The man said 'Yes', the woman said 'No'.

Hiscock, now angry, demanded an explanation and was told by the man that a woman called Mary or Molly was trapped in the forward part of the blazing boat.

He sent the strange couple below and sailed back to the fire. As the flames were approaching the foredeck he saw a bare-legged figure holding on to a davit. He lit another flare to try and light up the night and also to determine the figure which was obscured by smoke. As he rounded up to make his approach the woman down below stuck her head through the hatchway and said the attempt was futile. Hiscock ordered her below and closed the hatch and on his second approach told the second female to jump. She did so and she landed heavily across the cockpit coaming. Hiscock hauled her aboard.

She was uninjured although her face was blackened and her clothing singed. Hiscock sent her below and after getting *Wanderer II* hove-to went below himself.

'A curious sight met my eyes. Three nightmarish, smoke-grimed faces, grotesquely illuminated by the swinging lamp, made a strange contrast to the polished woodwork and the clean blue cushions'.

No-one was seriously hurt although the third passenger's legs were badly blistered.

Hiscock was understandably shaken up after his gallant rescue and his three new crew were yelling hysterically at one another. Hiscock broke out the rum and served a tot to each and took a draught himself.

He gave them blankets and offered his spare clothing to the bare-limbed female and went back on deck to discover the motor-cruiser had vanished. He supposed the fire had indeed reached her petrol tanks although no explosion was heard. He had arrived in the nick of time: the whole operation since first sighting the flames and the sinking of the motor-boat had lasted just one hour.

He now set a course for Plymouth to drop off his shipwrecked mariners ashore.

As he sailed on, the girl with the blistered limbs came up with soup for them both and Hiscock noticed how her companions were laid out on opposite bunks suffering from seasickness with a bowl between them. Yet the girl was not sick, had operated his Primus stove and was able to relieve Hiscock at the helm. Clearly of the three she appeared to have the most small-boat experience. He tried to find out what had happened but was too much of a gentleman to push his interrogation when she proved tight-lipped on names, times and other hard facts.

At dawn they drew Rame Head abreast and an hour later anchored in the Cattewater. Once at peace the sick passengers felt better, washed their faces and tucked into a full English breakfast. They then asked to borrow Hiscock's dinghy so that they could go ashore and use the telephone.

He launched his tender and all three clambered in and rowed ashore.

With commendable patience Hiscock sat aboard waiting for the dinghy to return and watching his fair wind blow uselessly up Channel.

By late afternoon he was tired of waiting and managed to hail a passing boatman to put him ashore.

He found his dinghy moored at the Barbican steps with no sign of his rescued mariners. So he simply rowed back out to *Wanderer II* and set sail once more. This modest and old-fashioned sailor did not want any passionate thank-you's, was not interested in the peculiar domestic arrangements which seemed to run as a subtext to the whole affair, but simply noted that they could have at least returned his dinghy and that a pair of singed shorts was a 'poor exchange for some excellent flannels'.

As both Hiscock and his wife Susan are now dead we may never know what on earth had happened before *Wanderer II* came across a blazing motor-cruiser that dark and rainy night near the Eddystone Light.

Bibliography: *Wandering Under Sail*, Eric Hiscock, Robert Ross & Co in association with George G. Harrap, revised and enlarged edition 1948.

SEA DARK, SKY CRYING

Isabelle Autissier, the only woman to compete in the 1994–95 BOC Challenge Round the World Singlehanded Race, was forced to abandon her crippled yacht deep in the Southern Ocean, and was plucked by helicopter at the limits of rescue services

It took just a split second and an unavoidable slam on the port side for Isabelle Autissier's dreams to suddenly come toppling down around her. A rigging screw on her yacht's main port shroud failed and the mast collapsed over the starboard side, snapped at the base.

It was 2 December and the 38-year-old French yachtswoman, a marine science professor and engineer, was halfway between Cape Town and the Kerguelen Islands on the seventh day of the second leg of the BOC Challenge Round the World Singlehanded Yacht Race.

Her 60 ft rocket ship *EPC2* had streaked away down the Atlantic from the September start in Charleston, South Carolina, America, to win a decisive victory in the first leg of the race, leaving the men, her fellow competitors, 1 200 miles astern battling in her wake for second place.

Now she was the southernmost boat in the fleet of 14 reduced from the 18 competitors who had begun the epic race.

'I felt like I had been hit in the stomach. I thought "No. Not this. Not here." It was already over for me. But what was the use of yelling, shouting and crying for a victory that was completely lost?' Isabelle asked herself.

She sent a message to Race HQ in Charleston: 'Dismasted. No danger immediately.' She was 1 200 miles from Cape Town, and lying at 48°52′S.

There was no time to waste. A mast can become a horrific hammer of carbon fibre threatening to puncture the hull of a yacht. The winch at the foot of the mast was already starting to smash a hole in the deck. With hacksaw, pliers and a knife, Isabelle scrabbled about on her knees cutting away the rig as the yacht rolled. She tried to save the boom, but it broke, dragged down by the weight of the mainsail.

Ninety minutes later, she had cut away most of the rig and stood on the bare deck of her yacht. She had one complete spinnaker pole and half of a broken one.

'There are 5 000 miles left to Sydney. I feel so much like crying for my lost hopes. But this is the way racing goes'.

At the crack of dawn next day, Isabelle began work afresh on erecting an emergency mast. Using her small 5-metre broken spinnaker pole, with a halyard rigged from the top, she raised the 9-metre pole.

'I am forgetting about the second leg. My goal is to arrive in Sydney with enough time to make preparations to start leg three with the others'.

Under two tiny headsails, Isabelle set course for Kerguelen Island, a remote French outpost some 1200 miles away that was home to weather and scientific research stations.

Two days later, when the sun was out, she worked to reinforce the base of her new mast with epoxy glue and carbon fibre. She wound a length of small diameter rope around the mast and glued it together to add thickness at the foot. In the damp conditions, to help it dry, she made a tent around the mast and used her small emergency generator inside to add warmth. *EPC2* was averaging four knots and was expected to arrive at Kerguelen Island in 13 days. Sources in France found a replacement mast for her yacht on Reunion Island that was shipped to Kerguelen on a French cargo vessel.

Two weeks later, sailing under jury rig, Isabelle, dubbed 'Isabelle the Incredible', arrived at Kerguelen Island eager to re-rig her yacht with the replacement mast.

It was snowing hard and the winds were over 40 knots as *EPC2* was towed into the protected harbour by a French scientific vessel conducting studies in the Antarctic region.

After a three-day stop at Kerguelen, Isabelle had converted *EPC2* from a single-masted sloop into a double-masted yawl, using her spinnaker pole as a mizzen mast. Twelve days later on 28 December, the 32nd day of leg two, Isabelle was averaging eight knots under bare poles with the wind howling around her at 60–70 knots.

She was at the back of the yacht in the narrow tunnel-like passage which linked the main cabin and the watertight aft compartment containing the yacht's steering systems.

'It was then that I heard it coming . . . like a powerful locomotive. I instinctively crouched down. I knew it was going to flatten the boat'. A rogue monster wave crashed over the yacht, launching it through a semipitchpole, end-over-end. At the same time the yacht did a corkscrew rollover through 360°. She was thrown onto the roof, choked by a rush of ice cold water. 'I could feel it rolling. I fell on the bulkhead, then on the ceiling, then on the other bulkhead. When I opened my eyes the boat was full of water. If I had been on deck I would have been washed away. It was very great for me that I was not there'.

The whole incident had lasted not more than 20 seconds. Isabelle crawled out of the tunnel and was speechless at what she saw. The yacht's cabin roof above the navigation station and her living quarters had disappeared. There was a gaping hole of five square metres where the carbon fibre coachroof had exploded under the water pressure. All she could see was forbidding grey sky and the sea washing in as waves continued to sweep the deck. The air pressure had plucked a lot of loose items out of the yacht in the rollover.

On deck, most of *EPC2's* jury masts and rigging had been swept away by the ocean. Isabelle's world had literally turned upside down

920 miles south-south-east of Adelaide. The boat was very low in the water, almost half submerged. She had to act quickly.

'A second wave would definitely finish us,' she thought. For two hours she bailed out as much water as possible using a bucket and stretched a sail over the gaping hole in the cabin roof, using a salvaged spar as a ridgepole for her makeshift 'tent'.

'All the steering systems were gone. The tiller had come away under pressure, leaving a hole which was leaking water into the once watertight rear compartment'.

The water temperature was freezing and the current was taking Isabelle further south, away from the nearest land. The air temperature was only 5°C with the wind chill factor sending even that plunging to −15°C. At first she thought she might try to go on. Her defiant optimism told her she might somehow rebuild the jury rig. Slowly reality dawned as fatigue took over. The steering system was destroyed. She was exhausted from sailing for three weeks with a jury rig.

'With the state of my boat and my personal state I knew it would not be safe to try and get to Sydney. I had to save what could be saved'. Two hours after the rollover, and for the first time in her seafaring life, Isabelle took out her distress beacons, two Alden 406 EPIRBs, and as night began to fall she switched them on.

Search and rescue operations were co-ordinated by Australia's MRCC in Canberra, while in France Isabelle's family were notified.

At Royal Australian Air Force bases near Sydney and Adelaide, flight crews were scrambled on long-range aircraft. A military search plane was on standby to fly to the yacht's last known position at first light next day.

As darkness fell on that first long night at sea, Isabelle, realising how far from land she was, knew that no rescue bid would be attempted until the next day. The forward watertight compartment, where her sails were stowed, was the only area on her stricken yacht not submerged in water and not structurally compromised. It was there that she sought refuge.

Lots of things had disappeared in the waves. The aft compartment was full of water and she didn't know if the rudders had gone because she had to shut the watertight doors to keep the boat afloat. She gathered clothes, food and survival gear, including a hand-operated desalinator for making drinking water, and moved into the forward compartment.

After the rollover this was to be her home for the next three days. She changed into her one-piece survival suit to try and conserve body warmth in the chilling conditions and wrapped a reflective foil space blanket around her.

It was a sleepless night for BOC race officials, as well as those on duty at Race HQ. All efforts to contact Isabelle by satellite messaging and long range radio had been in vain. From the slow drift of the EPIRB signals they knew something was badly wrong. Was Isabelle still with the yacht or in her life-raft? Or had the yacht sunk, leaving only the beacons afloat to transmit their bleak alarm?

Early next day a C-130 Hercules aircraft left Adelaide at 0400 on a mercy mission to find Isabelle and her yacht. The plane carried an extra passenger, Serge Viviand, head of Isabelle's shore support crew. The plane, equipped to drop life-rafts, handheld VHF radios and other survival gear, took four hours to reach the search area after a refuelling stop in Tasmania.

By dawn, Isabelle was already awake with the cold and had started work to clear the deck of broken rigging and spars ready for any rescue operation. She was tired and staggered around as the mastless yacht pitched and rolled in the heavy Southern Ocean swell. Suddenly she heard a distant rumble and looked up to see a plane flying overhead.

At around 0900 the plane had reached the search area. But sighting Isabelle was not easy. The positions given by the two distress beacons on board *EPC2* were sometimes as much as nine miles apart. And to make things even harder, from the skies above, the white deck of the stricken yacht was invisible against the backdrop of breaking wave crests. It took an agonising two hours and 50 minutes before the Hercules confirmed a visual sighting of the yacht. Isabelle on deck jumped up and down and waved to the search plane to show that she was uninjured. She was reported to be 'fit and well' and 'very near the location that her distress signal had begun transmitting'.

It had been an anxious 18-hour wait before the world knew that Isabelle Autissier was alive and still aboard her yacht.

'When I heard the plane it was a great moment for me,' said Isabelle. 'Communication was impossible because my radio was out of action. I sobbed with emotion'.

From the time they arrived, the Royal Australian Airforce never left Isabelle. Having found their needle in a haystack, they didn't want to risk losing her again. Military aircraft relayed every few hours and remained on station, like guardian angels, keeping a watch over her and monitoring the yacht's drift. The Hercules took some three hours to fly to her position and was able to stay four hours before flying back to refuel. An Orion PC3 antisubmarine aircraft also remained on vigil during daylight hours.

The Hercules plane, flying low over the water dropped an 11-person life-raft containing a handheld VHF radio. Isabelle had managed to secure it alongside the yacht.

Frustratingly for the rescue crew, Isabelle did not realise that the life-raft contained a radio for her to make contact with the plane's crew.

The second afternoon after being sighted, Isabelle located the radio and made voice contact with the crew of the Orion.

For the first time she learned that *HMAS Darwin* was en route to her position, having recalled its sailors from their Christmas holidays. She was also told of plans to lift her off her yacht by Darwin's on-board helicopter in two days' time.

She told the rescue plane that the rear compartment of *EPC2* was flooded and she had lost all steering capability. She added that she had plenty of food and water in her stores. The RAAF Orion PC3 aircraft crew arranged a regular radio schedule with Isabelle.

While Isabelle faced a wait of some 40 hours, she also started to come to terms with the impending separation from her yacht which had become such a part of her life after three years of work and thousands of miles.

31 December brought mixed emotions: relief that rescue was imminent, for she had been told that she would be lifted off her yacht by helicopter early that morning.

'An incredible acrobat was hanging from a rope. He made it onto the deck and put a harness around me and we were winched back up together'.

It was 0659 Sydney time on New Year's Eve. Three days after the rogue wave had overwhelmed her yacht, Autissier suddenly felt a great pang of sadness as she looked down on the heaving deck of *EPC2*.

So ended one of the most dramatic rescues in the history of ocean yacht racing.

* * *

This contains extracts from *The Loneliest Race, The Story of the 1994–95 BOC Around Alone Challenge,* by Paul Gelder, published by Adlard Coles Nautical, 1995.

THE FOUR RESCUES OF A SOLO ATLANTIC YACHTSMAN

Never-say-die yachtsman Trevor Wilson had retired before he started a series of attempts on the Atlantic which resulted in a quartet of rescues

Intrepid solo yachtsman Trevor Wilson, 70, a retired factory worker from Caernarfon, North Wales, is living proof of the dangers which lurk in the public library. After reading *Sailing To Freedom*, about the voyage from Stockholm to Norfolk, Virginia, of 16 men, women and children, all exiled Estonians, fleeing their Soviet-controlled country in 1945, Trevor's chances of a quiet retirement ended. Reading about the Estonians' hazardous 128-day voyage aboard a 36 ft double-ended sloop, *Erma*, was truly inspirational.

Trevor's first attempt to follow in his heroes' wake in 2000 was aboard an unsuitable boat: *Ozama*, a Trident 24. It ended in disaster when she lost her unsupported rudder in heavy weather 200 miles north of the

Azores. Trevor was adrift for three days before a Cypriot bulk carrier picked up his Mayday and rescued him from his abandoned boat.

Two years later Trevor was back with a better boat, *Vowden*, a Trintella 29, fitted with new chain plates, new rigging and a water-tight bulkhead in the forepeak. But this voyage was to bring the worst storm he ever experienced.

He set off from Plymouth and made good progress, but on the fifth day out the barometer went into freefall. 'The sky went a pinky, purple colour and the wind died away altogether. I dropped the mainsail and stowed it and awaited the wind under the headsail alone,' said Trevor.

He then bolted a DIY storm door across the companionway, using it as a sort of conning tower, 'I was to thank God I did that,' he said later.

Then the wind came up from the south-west and was soon blowing at gale force. As it increased to Force 9 Trevor lashed the tiller to leeward and rolled up the foresail to the size of a handkerchief. The boat lay at a 45 degree angle to the waves and was making about half a knot through the water.

Soon *Vowden* was being battered by gusts of 70 to 80 knots. Trevor later learned that round-the-world yachtswomen Dame Ellen MacArthur was in the same storm during the Route du Rhum 2002, which she described as being one of the toughest races of her career. Waves started breaking over the boat and a lot of water was cascading down below from beneath the main hatch, so Trevor stuffed towels beneath it.

But to get the water out of the boat Trevor had to go back on deck and lift up the cockpit side benches to get at the pump. This required waiting for a gap between waves and then quickly opening the hatch and clambering out.

It took 300 strokes to get the water out, but as he pumped, extra water poured in through the opened side benches. The wind was now screaming and the whole sea had turned white. Back down below he lay on the starboard bunk with a hand-bearing compass around his neck to check on her course.

Suddenly he was thrown out of his bunk with such a force it was like coming out of a cannon. 'Everything had gone quiet and I thought "Christ, she's turned over"'.

'I hit the teak cabin table and I could hear my ribs breaking and I felt excruciating pain in my left arm. Then the concertina-style doors of the head burst open and all my spare kit: sails, clothes, and bags came spewing out. Then she righted and I was thrown backwards and punched my head through a side locker and set off the brand new fire extinguisher'. Now, just to add to the confusion white powder was fizzing out all over the place and Trevor was choking for breath. With his one good arm he pulled back the hatch and threw the extinguisher over the side. Just then a huge sea knocked *Vowden* over on her beam ends and gallons of water poured down through the open hatch into the boat. This killed off all the electrics as the cabin lights went out. It was 2 am on day six.

'I forced myself out into the cockpit and was crouched down like a tortoise to get to the pump. I was wearing some ex-Army wet weather gear but the hood was designed to fit over a helmet and therefore kept blowing off. Every time I breathed it was as though somebody had stuck a knife in me. After 700 pumps I stopped counting'.

By dawn the wind had abated to about a Force 6. The cabin looked as though a bomb had hit it. On deck Trevor examined the damage. The stanchions on the port side were bent inboards and the cockpit floor gratings were jammed between them and the cockpit coaming. The starboard side dodger was ripped to shreds and the backstay was loose. His life-raft had been torn off the cabin top and was jammed between the starboard stanchions and the cabin side. Worst of all the self-steering paddle had torn off completely and was being towed astern by its lanyard like a drogue. The yoke which held it to the windvane was splayed out and Trevor tried using a G-clamp to jury-rig it without success.

He then discovered the galley cooker's knobs had seized solid and had to use a set of mole grips to turn them, but for fear of fracturing the gas pipe, he had to give up. He now faced the prospect of no warm drinks or food.

All his working charts were a pulp on the cabin sole. But using one which had not been damaged, he set a course for Crosshaven in Ireland, about 800 miles away.

'With the wind continuing south-west Force 6 I had half the genoa set and used shock cord either side of the tiller with a tin of baked beans hanging off the port side cord to get the boat steering north-east. She sailed for hour after hour like this and I managed to snatch some sleep during the day to be ready for the night when I kept a full lookout'.

After five days he saw a ship and called them up on his hand-held VHF and asked them to report his position to Falmouth Coastguard.

On the 15th night out the wind increased again, but by now he could see the flash of the Fastnet Rock lighthouse.

> I was getting very cold – especially my feet – so I cut the arms off my pullover and used the sleeves as socks, as everything else was soaked. I set a course for the Old Head of Kinsale The wind came up from east by north and started blowing Storm 10.
>
> I was now in fear of being blown back out into the Atlantic and as I didn't want to lose any ground I got the sea anchor out. It was now gusting 80 mph. After I bent the sea anchor to its cable the wind got hold of it, tore it from my grasp and took it up into the air like a kite!
>
> The sea-anchor immediately pulled her head down wind and I was paragliding back out into the Atlantic until it eventually crashed into the sea and pulled her head to wind, but not before I was pooped and another wave went crashing below.

At last Trevor had had enough and he sent out a Mayday on his hand-held VHF. It was picked up by a French trawler who called up the coastguard and Trevor was picked up by the Courtmacsherry lifeboat.

In Courtmacsherry hospital Trevor was treated for hypothermia, four broken ribs and a fractured left arm.

But still he refused to give up his attempt to follow the voyage of the exiled Estonians. His third attempt was in *Mykon*, a Cutlass 27, which he sailed from Port Dinorwic, North Wales in 2005. She crossed the Atlantic successfully and Trevor landed in Natal, Brazil. But she was later dismasted in a thunderstorm and wrecked on rocks off French Guyana. Trevor took to his life-raft and activated his EPIRB. He was picked up by a coastguard rescue craft eight hours later.

His fourth bid to get to Norfolk was in *Erma*, a £5 000 Warsash One Design, named after the yachts which had inspired all his adventures. On passage from Portland, Dorset to Virginia, USA she started leaking severely and lost her steering after three gales. Trevor said: 'The hull fractured around the starboard chain plates and I was taking on four gallons of water an hour. I was prepared to tolerate this but then the steering went and so I activated my EPIRB'.

A Portuguese military plane located him and dropped a green dye in the water so that a helicopter could find him. He was airlifted off the sinking *Erma* and landed in the Azores.

* * *

Reproduced with permission by *Yachting Monthly*.

PART EIGHT

Deliverance

THE EXPLODING WHALE

Crews on 19th century whaling ships earnt big pay or nothing depending on the success of their catch. So when a storm hit the *Cachalot* after she'd secured a precious sperm whale, the crew had to tend ship while the dead whale, lashed alongside, started to decay

The *Cachalot* was not a pretty ship, she was described by sailors as having come from a class of craft 'built by the mile and cut off in lengths as required'. It was difficult to tell her bow from her stern, her stumpy three masts stood up straight as broomsticks and her bowsprit looked as though it had been rigged by a child, standing as it did at a 45 degree angle. On the deck in the centre of this stubby, ungainly looking ship was what looked like a giant brick-built barbeque. For the *Cachalot* was a whaling ship from New Bedford, Massachusetts and her strange deck grill was used for rendering blubber to extract oil for lamps, especially the giant lamps used to warn ships away from rocky hazards along the coast. This ship sailed on three to four year voyages around the world hunting the sperm whale for this creature's valuable oil, as well as its spermaceti used for candles and ambergris, an ingredient used in the manufacture of perfume.

Although carrying only 400 tons she had a crew of 37, such was the labour involved in catching, cutting up and barrelling the oil. In comparison a clipper ship of 2 500 tons burthen had a crew of 28.

In the late 1890s Frank Bullen, an English sailor looking for a berth, found himself wandering the wharfs of New Bedford and was soon signed up for a whaling trip which would take him from New Bedford around the world via the Cape of Good Hope, the Indian Ocean, through the China Sea and on into Japanese waters and the Sea of Okhotsk, before sailing down through the Pacific around Cape Horn and home.

All the way they were hunting the sperm whale and before the voyage was over Bullen had been promoted to mate.

Towards the end of the voyage the *Cachalot* was looking for the 'bushy blow' of sperm whales in the Solander Grounds to the south of New Zealand. These were rich fishing grounds but crews had to face the persistent gales of the Southern Ocean where periods of fine weather are brief.

On one occasion having caught a sperm whale and towed it alongside in the whaling skiffs they were just about to start the process of cutting it up when a storm blew up. Loath to let the beast loose after all their hard work they shackled it alongside with chains and warps and tended to the ship's needs as they ran before the wind: hunter and hunted locked in a grim embrace. The huge carcass tore and strained at its fastenings and Bullen and his shipmates looked on hoping their ship would not be rent asunder.

Five other whaling ships were with them in similar situations and all scattered before the rising storm. All that day and night they ran before the tempest, checking the bilges for leaks. The next morning there was no sign of the weather improving, 'Indeed it looked like lasting a month,' Bullen recalled. Captain Count eyed the whale, gloomily apprehensive at the prospect of losing his latest catch.

By now the dead whale was beginning to swell up. Instead of its great bulk being just awash with most of its body below the surface it was now three feet above the seething waves and growing steadily larger as the gases of decomposition built up in its giant belly. 'Hour after hour went by without any change whatever, except in the whale, which, like some gradually-filling balloon, rose higher and higher, till at nightfall its bulk was appalling,' Bullen wrote in his log.

All through the second night of the storm the crew did little else but stare at their prey's increasing size, and by dawn the beast's 'bilge' or waterline rode level with the *Cachalot's* rail. As the ship rolled to leeward in the huge seas the whale 'towered above the deck like a mountain'.

Fascinated by the strange spectacle Bullen and his shipmates watched and waited until suddenly 'with a roar like the bursting of a dam, the pent-up gases tore their furious way out of the distended carcass, hurling the entrails in one horrible entanglement widespread over the sea'.

It was just as well the exploding whale had been on the leeward side of the ship otherwise she would have been covered from truck to keel in rotting whale flesh, but even so the 'unutterable fetid smell wrought its poisonous way back through that fierce, pure blast, permeating every nook of the ship with its filthy vapour until the stoutest stomach there protested in unmistakable terms against such vile treatment'.

A crestfallen Captain Count now had 17 m of worthless blubber threatening to rip his ship apart and so he ordered the corrupt mass to be cut adrift and the ship fought the gale for a further five days driving ever further down into the Southern Ocean.

When the wind eventually eased and shifted to the south they blew back to Port William in New Zealand's Stewart Island, without a whale.

DOWNHILL RACER

The fastest woman to cross the Atlantic, Clare Francis gave up the hard facts of the sea for a life of fiction as a best-selling crime writer

She was born in a county without a coastline yet went on to become the fastest woman to sail solo across the Atlantic in 1976 racing her Ohlson 38 ft boat *Robertson's Golly* in the OSTAR from Plymouth to Newport in 29 days.

The following year, Clare Francis, from Surrey, the young woman who gave up a promising career in the City to go sailing, set off as the only woman skipper in the epic Whitbread round-the-world race. Helping her sail the 65 ft *ADC Accutrac* were two women and nine men.

Before the second leg, which took them into the Southern Ocean, all the crews were given a briefing in the stopover port of Cape Town. They were reminded about the importance of clipping on with their harnesses every time they went on deck as anyone going overboard would be as good as dead. The boats would be cork-screwing at vast speeds downwind in front of westerly gales. To stop and turn round let alone find the victim was a daunting task. Also, if they lost the boat they were warned that the chances of survival in such seas, thousands of miles from land in freezing temperatures in a life-raft would not be high.

After suffering a broach – in which the boat goes sideways on to the waves and is pushed down so that her mast gets close to the sea – Clare was unsurprisingly nervous, especially at night when sailing was much more difficult as the seas could not be judged and the boat was sailed on instruments alone. She and her crew were learning the art of surfing: keeping the boat straight as a 40 ft wave came up from astern, lifted her up onto its crest and into the full force of the wind, which then took over as the dominant power and pushed her like a toboggan down the face of the wave in a welter of spray to the trough beneath. Speeds of up to 20 knots were attained, but always there was the fear of broaching in such conditions and often the spinnaker went billowing out of control, dragged off to one side or another and threatening to drag the boat over on her side, rather than pulling the boat from straight ahead.

During one gybe they split the mainsail in two: it had worn thin through chafing against the rigging. The sail was unbent, taken below and replaced with a new one. It took many days to repair the rent.

With such huge loads on the rig, there were accidents. One crewman had the skin on the palms of his hands burnt open as dozens of feet of hard, nylon sheet slipped through his hands when he misjudged taking a rope off a winch. Another crewman was flicked 15 feet off the deck on a headsail sheet. But these were minor incidents compared to the accident which had happened to another competing boat, *GB II*. They heard the chastening news via the ship's radio. Once again it was the spinnaker, the boat's most difficult sail to handle – and the most dangerous in such conditions – which caused the near fatal accident. While the boat was in a trough the sail collapsed, denied the wind behind a mound of sea. The ropes which controlled it dropped too, like the lines which animate a marionette. Two crewmen working the sail on deck unwittingly stood in a benign loop of one of the sail's guy ropes. As the boat rode up on the next wave, the sail filled and the benign rope became a lethal lasso crushing the legs of one man, Rob James, and, more seriously, trying to cut the second man, Nick

Dunlop, in two as the noose was around his waist. After the contents of his stomach were forced out through his mouth the victim's tongue was pushed out: a swollen gobbet of meat. His circulation was stopped and his eyes were bulging out of their sockets having turned crimson. Other crewmen managed to cut the line before he was crushed to death.

Tragically just six years later, Rob James, husband of Naomi James, the first woman to sail single-handed around the world via Cape Horn, was lost overboard – not in a demanding race in the Southern Ocean – but while cruising off Salcombe in Devon.

Clare and her crew finished the race fifth out of 15 boats after 27 000 gruelling miles. Once two books on her sailing adventures were written, Clare turned her back on the sea and settled down to a life of novel writing becoming an international best seller.

THE FIRST MAN TO SAIL ROUND THE WORLD ALONE

American master mariner Joshua Slocum became a household name when he proved that a lone sailor and a small boat could circle the globe

Retired sea captain Joshua Slocum was 51 when he rigged out an old 37 ft oyster smack, *Spray*, and set off from Boston, Massachusetts to sail around the world on his own. *Spray*, a yawl, had great beam, and a long keel which enabled her to be left to sail herself for long distances. But she also had a vice, which experts believe may have led to the great sailor's death: her shallow draught.

After his voyage Slocum became a rich man thanks to his writings and lectures, but before it he had to make ends meet and *Spray* was a craft whose original shell was a century old. For a dinghy he used an old fishing dory which doubled up as a washing-machine and a bath-tub. To help work out his longitude he used an ancient tin clock which he occasionally dipped in boiling water to help it function.

His first port of call after leaving America was the Azores where he obtained fresh stores including cheese and plums. Soon afterwards he became delirious and lay in agony on the cabin floor while the self-steering *Spray* held her course for Gibraltar from where he intended to cross the Mediterranean and enter the Suez Canal. But he was advised against this route because of the threat from Moorish pirates. So instead he headed back across the Atlantic, and was overhauled by a pirate felucca anyway. As Slocum reefed, the felucca broached in a squall and was dismasted, tangling with *Spray* and breaking her boom. Slocum luffed *Spray* into the wind and furled the mainsail to prevent it being torn by the spar and brought his rifle on deck to defend himself. The pirates were too busy to bother with the chase any longer.

After further adventures Slocum entered the Strait of Magellan at the bottom of South America to face head winds, but also more peril from the natives. To convince watching locals he was not alone he rigged a dummy figure on deck, went down into the cabin after having shown himself, changed his clothes as he went forward and emerged out of the fore-hatch as a 'third' man.

At night before turning in he spread carpet-tacks, points uppermost, on the deck. On one occasion he was woken by the yells of natives as they put their bare soles on the tacks. He rushed on deck with his rifle and fired at the intruders, who had retreated to their canoes.

At the island of Juan Fernandez Slocum found settlers and taught them the art of cooking doughnuts.

After a voyage of 72 days Slocum made landfall at Nukuhiva, one of the Marquesas Islands and later landed on one of the Samoan Islands. Here he met Mrs Stevenson, the widow of Robert Louis Stevenson, author of *Treasure Island*.

From Sydney, Australia he sailed inside the Great Barrier Reef to Thursday Island, on to the Cocos-Keeling Islands, Rodriguez and across the Indian Ocean to Port Natal, Durban. Here Slocum was visited by three Boer scholars who were preparing a work to support the contention of President Kruger that the world was flat. When he arrived at Cape Town he left the *Spray* and made a trip to Pretoria. He was presented to President Kruger by a judge who said Slocum was sailing round the world. This upset Kruger, who said the judge meant that Slocum was sailing along the world!

At St Helena Slocum was given a goat. As soon as the animal had found its sea-legs it ate the mariner's chart of the West Indies. Then a treecrab he was bringing from the Cocos-Keeling Islands broke out of its box and tore his sea-jacket while the goat devoured his straw hat. Upon reaching Ascension, Slocum landed the goat. To prove that he sailed alone Slocum had the vessel inspected when he was ready to sail and secured a certificate from the officials, who fumigated her to make sure that no one was hiding below.

He then sailed towards Brazil and spoke to an American warship, which signalled that war had broken out between Spain and the United States, but the *Spray* was not stopped by any Spanish vessels. As he approached the West Indies Slocum was worried by the lack of the chart which the goat had eaten. He was alarmed one night by what he took to be the white flash of seas breaking on a reef, and despite all his efforts he could not weather them. At last the *Spray* was tossed high by the seas and then Slocum was able to see that the flash came from the lighthouse on the island of Trinidad.

From Antigua he sailed for the shores of New England, getting into a sea in the Gulf Stream that proved too much for his worn rigging. He nearly lost his mast when the jibstay broke; but he climbed the mast and managed to secure it. He was almost home when a tornado that had caused havoc in New York City struck the *Spray*, but the alert Slocum had not closed his weather eye. The boat was under bare poles with everything snug and a sea-anchor out when the storm reached the little ship.

Newport Harbour, Rhode Island, was mined, yet the *Spray*'s shallow draught enabled Slocum to sail her close to the rocks avoiding the ordnance and so into the port. He arrived on 27 June 1898, having sailed more than 46 000 miles in three years, two months and two days. A little later he sailed the *Spray* to Fairhaven, and moored her where she had been launched.

In November 1909, Slocum set sail for the West Indies on one of his usual winter voyages and was never seen again.

Later Howard I. Chapelle, curator of maritime history at the Smithsonian Institute in Washington, and an expert on small sailing-craft, demonstrated that *Spray*, while stable in most conditions, could capsize if heeled beyond a relatively shallow angle. His analysis was that Slocum was merely lucky that his boat had not killed him earlier.

NOT QUITE THE FASTEST SHIP

Britain's *Cutty Sark* was built to sail tea home from China in the fastest possible time. She made some record runs but had a serious competitor from the USA – *Thermopylae*

On Monday 21 May 2007 a flickering orange glow was reflected in the early morning windows of waterside Greenwich. One of London's most famous landmarks and major tourist attractions was burning down. The clipper ship *Cutty Sark* was gutted by the fire started by a dust extractor which had been left plugged in over the weekend. Fortunately most of the important parts of the ship had already been dismantled as she was undergoing restoration. But she lost much of her deck planking and side planking. Ironically it had been her decks which held her back from winning outright the accolade of becoming the fastest sailing ship in the world. This was because the original timber was made of heavy and hard-wearing teak, whereas the decks of her greatest rival *Thermopylae* were built of the lighter yellow pine.

Both ships had been built for the tea trade; it was economically important and, for reasons of prestige, desirable to be the first ship back to the UK with the new season's cuppas from China. Also, this is why these two beautiful ships were built (before the opening of the Suez Canal ended the tea clipper business).

The *Thermopylae* was built first, in 1868, the *Cutty Sark* being designed in the following year to beat her. Both were composite: iron frames planked over with wood and both had a displacement of 1 970 tons at load draught. The dimensions of the *Thermopylae* were 212 feet between perpendiculars, 36 feet beam by 21 feet depth of hold; those of the *Cutty Sark* were the same, but with 6 ins more length. The *Thermopylae* has often been regarded as the faster ship in lighter winds, but the *Cutty Sark* came into her own in a blow.

In 1875–76 the two ships arranged an outward race, the *Cutty Sark* leaving London for Sydney nine days before the *Thermopylae* sailed for Melbourne. But a collision at the beginning of the voyage which cut down the *Cutty Sark's* sail area, and a captain who could not crack on sail in the manner of the old-timers, resulted in her passage being 75 days against the *Thermopylae's* 68. Home with tea, the *Cutty Sark* made a passage of 108 days and the *Thermopylae* one of 125, but the Glen Line steamer in the same service, was home in 42 days via the Suez Canal. In 1877 the position was reversed, the *Thermopylae* completing the passage from Shanghai in 102 days against the *Cutty Sark's* 127. Outward bound later in the year, the *Cutty Sark* was damaged by a collision in a gale, but she still managed 72 days to Sydney against *Thermopylae's* 74 to Melbourne. The two ships raced again from Sydney to Shanghai with coal, the *Cutty Sark* taking 40 days and the *Thermopylae* 48.

They were both again in rivalry on the Australian wool trade in the 1880s and under Captain Richard Woodget, *Cutty Sark* won the wool race ten years out of ten beating *Thermopylae* every time they met. *Cutty Sark* posted Australia-to-Britain times of as little as 67 days, and in one instance outsailed the fastest steamship there then was, *RMS Britannia*. Her best run, 360 nautical miles (666 km) in 24 hours was said to have been the fastest of any ship of her size.

In 1895 *Thermopylae* was sold to the Portuguese Navy to be converted into the training ship *Pedro Nunes*, and she seldom left the River Tagus. Seven years later she was made a target for torpedo practice and sunk in October 1907.

In 1922 *Cutty Sark* was bought by Captain Wilfred Dowman, who restored her and used her as a training ship in Greenhithe, Kent. In 1954 she was moved to a custom-built dry-dock at Greenwich.

After the fire which almost destroyed her, Richard Doughty, the chief executive of the Cutty Sark Trust, revealed that at least half of the fabric of the ship had not been on site as it had been removed during the preservation work. He estimated the blaze had upped the restoration cost by £5–10 million, bringing the total cost of the ship's restoration to £30–35 million. With such sums being debated one lobby called for her to thrill again: not as a static object but as a sailing ship.

That call has been ignored: the *Cutty Sark* will achieve a bigger gate as part of the Greenwich skyline than as a ship which sails. She will be mounted on a glass 'sea' and visitors will be able to walk beneath the keel that once cleaved the waters off Cape Horn.

A large hole will be cut out below the waterline in the ship's starboard quarter, to let the punters in.

There are no shellbacks left alive today to give their verdict of the clipper pinned to the Greenwich promenade like a rare butterfly.

THE FIRST MAN TO SAIL ROUND THE WORLD NON-STOP AND ALONE

Sir Robin Knox-Johnston was the first man to complete a solo circumnavigation without stopping. He is Britain's greatest living sailor

On 22 April 1969 a battered white sailing boat with orange rust streaks running down her hull, patches in her sails and green slime around her waterline entered Falmouth Harbour and was boarded by Customs officers, one of whom, while trying to keep a straight face asked her skipper: 'Where from?'

'Falmouth,' came the reply from the lean, tough-looking man clad in filthy yellow oilskins.

Robin Knox-Johnston had become the first human being to sail alone and non-stop around the world: he had set out from Falmouth 313 days and 30 000 miles ago.

Today many men, after such an ordeal, would be rushed away for psychological assessment and counselling before being presented to the media.

Knox-Johnston simply stepped ashore waved both hands in the air and – on legs unsteady after such an incarceration – wobbled off for a hot bath, a hot steak and a cold beer.

But his achievement was monumental. The boat, *Suhaili*, a tough old 32 ft ketch-rigged slowcoach, heavily built in teak, looked like a mini-Victorian workhouse below. She was devoid of luxury; a Spartan shed-like space where a large vice took up as much room as the stove.

She had wallowed around the most dangerous waters in the world at the walking pace of a human being: four miles an hour and Knox-Johnston had been faced with every trial imaginable. These included diving over the side to plug gaps in her leaking timbers and dispatching an over-inquisitive shark with a round from his 303 rifle.

He faced polluted fresh water tanks, the wrecking of his radio after a storm, the disintegration of his self-steering gear and the breakages of boom and tiller.

He also ran aground and had to jump over the side and wade off with his anchor, dropping it in deeper water so he could haul off when the tide rose.

He had left Falmouth to take part in the *Sunday Times* Golden Globe round the world race but returned to discover that he was the only one of the nine starters still in the competition. All the others had either dropped out or in one case been wrecked. And it was then he learned also of the tragic death of fellow competitor Donald Crowhurst, who is believed to have committed suicide by casting himself into the sea from the decks of his trimaran *Teignmouth Electron*.

Knox-Johnston – then not a wealthy man – had no hesitation in presenting his race winnings £5 000 – more than £60 000 in today's money – to Crowhurst's widow, Clare, which resulted in her being able to keep her heavily mortgaged house to bring up their four children.

The stores Knox-Johnston took with him included 8 612 tins of food, 14 pounds of curry powder, 24 pounds of cashew and peanuts, 3 000 cigarettes, 120 cans of lager, and 24 bottles of whisky and brandy. He also stowed below 18 loo rolls. History does not record if he ran out or not and as he was knighted in 1995 nobody has since dared ask.

In 1989, Sir Robin sailed *Suhaili* across the Atlantic following Christopher Columbus' route and using only a basic astrolabe for navigation. He reached San Salvador after 3 000 miles of sailing. He later sailed her to Greenland with climber Chris Bonington to climb a virgin peak in the Arctic.

After this *Suhaili* was put on display in the National Maritime Museum, Greenwich, but the air conditioning was a greater threat to the boat's timbers than any Southern Ocean wave. After two years her timbers were drying out dangerously and Sir Robin had her re-launched and is still sailing her to this day.

DELIVERANCE TRIP

He became a byword in confessing to slip-ups at sea. It all began for Des Sleightholme one cold winter on the East Coast

A skipper of the old school, Des Sleightholme became an instructor in seamanship at the Outward Bound Sea School taking the 50-ton Edwardian schooner *Hoshi* and the Brixham trawler *Provident* around the Channel Islands, and into the Bay of Biscay through the Chenal du Four and the Raz de Sein.

But such seamanship was hard learned from his first days as a fledgling delivery skipper.

One of his first jobs almost ended in disaster. It was February 1948 just three years after World War II had ended and many creeks, rivers and scruffy old boatyards were full of craft which had been laid up before the conflict and untouched for years. Some of these craft were owned by servicemen who never returned home.

One such craft was a ketch-rigged converted lifeboat lying at Burnham-on-Crouch, Essex. Des and his crew got the job of sailing her round to Emsworth for £50. At Burnham the pair rowed out to the boat which was lying in mid-stream.

'Her lifeboat hull had been raised to form what looked like a bus shelter; she had a bowsprit with a slack bobstay and her mainmast was raked so far forward that any seagull perching there, and being so minded, could have hit the bowsprit four times out of five'.

The boat was leaking: bilge water was already over the floorboards and the ex-lorry engine fired up immediately – a sign that the boatyard proprietor had been out just before the delivery crew arrived and had the ancient machine running to make sure it would start.

They decided to start the following morning and negotiate the sandbanks of the East Coast in daylight. A miserable damp and cold night was spent aboard and after a hurried breakfast cooked on a Primus stove they set the mainsail and jib and dropped the mooring just as it started to snow.

They had with them their own compass – a former RAF grid compass – in a wooden box which had lost its fluid: the compass card in the bowl lay 'motionless as a dead crow in a chimney,' Des remarked. The vessel had a seized up Walker log and an old sash window weight bent onto a piece of codline for a lead.

They took the ebb out of the River Crouch and having threaded through the estuary sands found themselves at dusk between the Tongue Light Vessel and the flare of the North Foreland light with their south-west wind backing to the south.

As the wind freshened to Force 4 to 5 they reefed her down and hove her to on occasion to bail out the leaking dinghy. It was so cold they took one-hour watches and rigged up steering lines to the tiller so she could be helmed from below.

They picked up the North Goodwin Lightship before the visibility went completely, leaving Des trying to make sense of their position with his malfunctioning navigation tools. Then the mizzen sail split in two followed shortly by the jib. The old, cotton sails were rotten.

Under just reefed mainsail and staysail the boat carried lee helm and they found it impossible to tack her: she just fell back off the wind and went stern first. So they had to gybe the boat round on each tack and by now the topsides – laying over in the seas – were leaking so badly she needed bailing out every half hour. They tried caulking the planks with melted soap, but that did not help much.

They were lucky not to run into trouble before daylight showed them they were headed straight for the Goodwin Sands. By the time they realised their predicament there was not enough sea room to make the clumsy manoeuvre of gybing her round so they started the engine and opened the throttle right out to get the boat round and on the other tack away from danger.

The sudden burst of activity from the engine caused the unlagged exhaust pipe to glow almost red hot which in turn caught fire to odds and ends of spare line in the aft locker.

The petrol tank was situated just above the conflagration. Fortunately the pair put out the blaze and managed to limp into Dover Harbour where they spent three days sorting the boat out and waiting for a fair wind. Setting off once more they next lost the dinghy in overfalls off Dungeness. The leaky hull had filled with water and upon being snubbed to attention as the old lifeboat surfed down a wave, broke loose. Des and his pal were left towing just the dinghy's stem!

The fire-blackened hull and the lost dinghy had the new owner's 'great flabby chin shaking with fury' when they eventually arrived at Emsworth.

But Des never forgot the lessons learned on that passage and along with many others came to share them with the readership of *Yachting Monthly* magazine many years later, after his mate in life and also on board – Joyce – gave birth to their daughter Michelle and he decided to come ashore and find a job. He became editor of *YM* in 1967 having worked under the equally legendary Maurice Griffiths, and ran the magazine for 18 years.

His conclusion about this ill-fated trip was made with characteristic Des candidness: 'That we were totally irresponsible and ignorant is beyond any question. It is easy to lay blame on the boat. A seaman – a good delivery skipper, for instance – takes a long, hard look at the boat, her gear and her installations before he ever leaves harbour and we did none of those things'.

THE SHIP THAT SAILED HERSELF

Some vessels are so well balanced they will sail themselves. This barge was abandoned by her crew but sailed on, even crossing a reef and beaching herself unharmed in a rock-strewn archipelago

On shore a white Christmas is a magical event beloved by one and all. Afloat there is little romance attached to a white out. On Christmas Day 1928 the Thames sailing barge *Lady Daphne* was on passage from Weymouth to Fowey where a cargo awaited her. Late in the day a north-easterly gale sprang up and her three crew shortened sail as the wind increased bringing snow with it. As the barge was 'light' – not loaded – her freeboard was considerable so the sea running that night must have been enormous – probably as the flood tide turned against the gale – for in those blizzard conditions a huge unseen wave burst out of the driving snow onto her deck and washed the skipper over the side.

The mate and third hand struggled as the barge became unmanageable and continued to run before the maelstrom down Channel. The two remaining crew used paraffin, kept aboard for the navigation lights, to soak rags and burn them off as flares, but their distress calls went unnoticed in the snow until they passed the signal station on the Lizard.

The Lizard lifeboat was called out and 12 miles south-west of the Lizard in the early hours of Boxing Day the two half-frozen men leapt from the deck of the barge to safety. They had used the last of the paraffin to burn an old coat just before their deliverance. Had this not been seen they would have been left to their fate aboard the *Lady Daphne*.

However, as things turned out it wasn't the barge that would have let them down.

Built in 1923 by Shorts of Rochester, the *Lady Daphne* had the unusual distinction of being built from lines: most barges were built by eye or from half models. This certainly helped with her handling capabilities and she was a fast barge into the bargain.

The *Lady Daphne* sailed on and as the wind backed into the south-east and blew even harder, by the afternoon of Boxing Day she was approaching the Isles of Scilly where an officer of the Black Watch regiment, second-lieutenant Bernard Fergusson, was enjoying his Christmas break. There had been a run of bad weather and no less than four ships had grounded on the rocks of the islands in the last two weeks. So when the sails of a vessel were seen approaching the islands through the latest tempest there was considerable interest and the officer climbed the watch tower at Tresco Abbey with another witness to watch events unfold.

Lady Daphne, her sails – apart from the jib on the bowsprit end – in ribbons, was making her way to Crowe Sound, a dangerous passage at that state of the tide and breakers through it were clearly visible. But a barge only draws the width of a domestic house door when light and she sailed straight through without touching. The St Mary's lifeboat had been called and was on the way to her. But the sea was running so high that neither vessel could see the other. But the two men atop the watch tower could witness the operation with the advantage of their elevation.

A jumble of gear just in front of the wheel looked, to the men, like an unconscious sailor lashed to the barge which explained to them why she did not turn south to the safety of St Mary's Pool, but stood straight on for the Hats, which she hit, but staggered across into the deeper water on the leeward side. It was at this point the lifeboatmen got aboard her and adjusted her helm and just as they did so her jib split in two with a crack like the sound of a gun. *Lady Daphne* was having none of it. She'd sailed all this way on her own and she now beached herself on Tresco beach. Because of her skilful negotiation of Crowe Sound the lifeboatmen thought she must have a man aboard with local knowledge. Instead they were amazed to find the only living creature aboard was the captain's canary.

Lady Daphne was eventually towed to Hugh Town where she was given a temporary repair before being towed back to the mainland for a full overhaul.

She is still sailing to this day and can be seen regularly at her berth in St Katharine's Dock in London.

ROUND THE WORLD IN 1 000 BREAKAGES

Many yachtsmen today are quick to call upon the rescue services when things go wrong. Frenchman Alain Gerbault solved his own problems as he endlessly sailed alone around the world

The French yachtsman, linguist and champion lawn-tennis player, Alain Gerbault, abandoned his profession as a civil engineer, to sail *Firecrest* a 39 ft gaff-rigged yacht round the world. Like her owner *Firecrest* was long and thin. And while the wiry fitness of the skipper was an asset to ocean voyaging, the narrow beam of *Firecrest* was not. She was a Victorian racing cruiser, plank-on-edge type, flush-decked, of heavy displacement, the sort of boat in calm weather which would bob up and down in her own hole creating endless wear and tear. Designed by Dixon Kemp, and built by P. T. Harris at Rowhedge,

Essex, in 1892, *Firecrest's* overall length was 39 feet, her beam 8 ft 6 in, and her draught 7 feet. She had a lead keel weighing three and a half tons, with another three tons of internal ballast.

Gerbault sailed *Firecrest* from Southampton to the French Riviera and spent a year sailing in the Mediterranean before setting out single-handed from Cannes in April, 1923, to Gibraltar.

He was soon busy with repairs. The gooseneck holding the boom to the mast broke; a topping lift parted; and then his jib halyard gave way and spilled the jib into the sea.

On 15 May Gerbault anchored at Gibraltar. After an overhaul of gear he left Gibraltar on 6 June, but before he'd left the Straits a gale blew his jib to pieces.

Next day the patent roller-reefing gear, which had been repaired at Gibraltar, failed because of a fracture; and the mainsail began to part at the seams; thus before he was two days out of Gibraltar he was busy repairing his mainsail.

Because the galley was in the fo'c'sle he found the pitch and roll too much for the gimbaled stove, so that pots and pans continually rolled off.

Next the bobstay, running from the end of the bowsprit to the stem, broke, and he had to go out to the end of the bowsprit to repair it. Then the foot of the mainsail ripped.

Near Madeira the trade wind fell off. During the calms that followed, Gerbault experimented with his sails and found that by furling the mainsail, setting the trysail and trimming the jib in flat he could get *Firecrest* to hold her course unaided by the tiller. He was therefore able to sail round the clock, although the speed under this rig was reduced.

Before long, various parts of the wire rigging gave trouble. Gerbault found that for many purposes rope was better than steel wire, because rope will bear jerks and jolts much better than wire.

One sea that broke aboard the *Firecrest*, burying her deck under tons of water, broke her bowsprit and caused part of the rigging to give way, so that *Firecrest* was in danger of dismasting.

After repairing both he was determined to make for New York, which he eventually reached 101 days out from Gibraltar. In New York the boat was fitted with a new Oregon pine bowsprit, new standing rigging, new sails, a bronze bobstay, a hollow boom and new roller-reefing gear. The original gaff mainsail was replaced by a triangular one.

Sailing from New York in November 1924 Gerbault met bad weather almost from the start. On 5 November, when he had not seen a vessel for two days, he saw that his port light was out, and went below to re-fill the lamp with paraffin. Before he could get the light re-shipped a steamer scraped the bowsprit of the *Firecrest*. The force of the blow tore the bitts out of her foredeck and broke the forestay and the jibstay, so that the mast threatened to go overboard at any moment. Gerbault carried out temporary repairs, but had an anxious time in the gales that battered the yacht before she anchored in the harbour of St George, Bermuda.

The crippled yacht had been reduced to a sorry state in little more than a fortnight. And as he had set out before stretching his new sails the gales had spoiled the set of the mainsail, which had to be recut.

Much of the work done in New York had to be repeated in Bermuda as well as the recaulking of the hull, which meant that the copper sheathing had to be raised and then hammered down again.

The repairs took three months before Gerbault sailed for Colon, the Atlantic entrance to the Panama Canal. He was towed through the Canal, and spent some time at Balboa, on the Pacific side where he met the second man to sail around the world solo: Harry Pidgeon, a Los Angeles photographer, who was concluding his voyage in the 34 ft yawl *Islander*, which he'd built himself.

Thirty-seven days out of Panama, he reached Chatham Island, in the Galapagos, some 800 miles from Panama. Here he obtained water and fruit, and prepared for the long sail of 3 000 miles to the Gambier Archipelago.

Gerbault ran south, losing the trade wind in a week of calm. When the wind returned the rigging was in such a bad state that he lost his backstay, both topping lifts, six masthoops, and the oak tiller snapped. After 49 days at sea Gerbault anchored in the harbour of Rikitea. In the months he spent with the natives Gerbault learnt their language, and then sailed 1 000 miles north to the Marquesas, where he made many Polynesian friends. He sailed on to the coral islands of the Tuamotu group, and so to Tahiti and Bora Bora. But it was at Wallis Island that Gerbault suffered his next gear failure. A borrowed anchor (he had previously lost his own) failed to prevent *Firecrest* dragging on to a reef in a gale. Her three-ton lead keel was torn off and Gerbault was swimming to the shore when, relieved of the weight of the keel, the *Firecrest* floated over the top of the reef and joined her skipper on the beach, digging a berth for herself in the sand.

Gerbault took all the ballast out and moved his personal belongings to the homes of friends ashore. With the aid of natives the yacht was righted and shored up. A barge was floated over the keel, lashed to it at low water, and lifted off on the next tide. After many weeks a steamship with a forge aboard entered the lagoon, and the chief engineer made two iron bolts and four bronze bolts out of an old propeller shaft for *Firecrest's* keel.

Once the *Firecrest* was repaired Gerbault put to sea again. On arriving at Suva, in the Fiji Islands, he had the *Firecrest* hauled up on a slipway, and further repairs were made. After having left Fiji, Gerbault continued his voyage passing through the Torres Strait, north of Australia. Here he nearly came to grief in the reef-strewn waters when his anchor chain parted, after he had lost his kedge anchor because of the warp snapping. A native sloop towed him to Coconut Island where Gerbault managed to borrow an anchor on condition he left it at Thursday Island for the owner's friends to collect. Gerbault obtained ground tackle at Thursday Island and sailed clear of the reefs. He then sailed on to the Cocos Keeling Islands, where he saw the remains of the famous German raider *Emden*.

Gerbault then journeyed across the Indian Ocean to Rodriguez, and for the first time trusted himself to a pilot. The *Firecrest* touched the coral in a narrow channel, as the pilot had not realised that a deep-keeled yacht carries considerable way. But *Firecrest* was undamaged.

At the next island, Reunion, he had various ironwork repaired, in preparation for the rough passage to Durban. In Cape Town, Gerbault drydocked *Firecrest*, finding that teredo worm had eaten away part of the rudder stock.

He rounded the Cape of Good Hope and via St Helena and Ascension Island, made his way to the Cape Verde Islands. Porto Grande, the chief harbour in the group, is in the island of St Vincent, which is separated from the island of St Antonio by a channel a few miles wide through which the trade wind blows with some force, raising a strong current.

After many attempts at the channel, Gerbault became exhausted and as the wind fell light, he fell asleep only waking up when *Firecrest* hit a reef a few yards from the beach of St Antonio. A hole had been knocked in her side, but this was plugged, and, with a crew manning a line of buckets to keep her afloat, she was towed across the channel to Porto Grande. Here she was repaired and Gerbault sailed, but she leaked so badly that he turned back and decided to stay at St Vincent for some months, superintending repairs and writing a book.

She still leaked badly both on passage to the Azores and during the final leg to Le Havre, northern France which he reached in July 1929.

It had taken six years and 40 000 miles, but endless repairs.

The next time Gerbault put to sea it was in a new boat.

DIY OCEAN RACER

He re-mortgaged his home four times, cannibalised old bangers to stay on the road and once salvaged and re-built lawnmowers to earn a crust. Dick Durham meets the greatest eccentric of sailing's Formula 1

Aged 18 Steve White learned to ride horses, worked as a stable boy and nursed a dream to become a champion jockey. But he grew too big for the saddle and it was surf not turf that gained him his spurs. His steed was an Open 60 and the going was rough: racing round the globe in the world's toughest race.

At Dorchester South railway station a turquoise Alpha Romeo 2.4 litre turbo estate pulled up in a cloud of dust. The boyish face of Steve White, 36, framed in blonde curls, peered through the windscreen. He cleared papers, and a laptop off the passenger seat and I climbed in. Soon we were curving round the bends of Dorset at an alarming speed.

Knowing he had put together his Vendée Globe, solo, non-stop, round-the-world race challenge on a shoestring, I questioned Steve's choice of car. 'A friend gave it to me. It's worth £1 500. That's too much to have invested in a car. So I'm selling it and will buy a banger for £200'. The rest will go towards the bill for upgrading his Open 60 *Toe In the Water* for further offshore races.

We pulled up alongside two cannibalised Saab saloons parked in the road outside Steve's three-bed semi, a few miles north of Dorchester, which he re-mortgaged four times to pay for his Vendée Globe campaign. The cars sit on flat tyres: a project awaiting attention from Steve, a former mechanic.

He freed the battered garden gate, held to its post with string, and three tail-wagging dogs: Sparky, a lurcher, Tweed, a collie and Poppy a Jack Russell vied for the chance to lick him. The back garden is habitat to even more creatures: 13 rabbits, three ducks, two guinea pigs and a goose which wander among spare car bumpers, discarded kid's bicycles and deck gear which Steve is restoring for use on *Toe in the Water*. He shares the home with Kim, his wife, their four children: Jason, 20, Eryn, 16, Isaac, 9 and seven-year-old Euan, as well as six cats who sleep in baskets on the stairs. Tropical fish glide back and forth in a living room aquarium which reflects a dining table strewn with half-repaired computers, disembowelled mobile phones, and discarded hi-fi equipment.

What seems like the domestic chaos of a mad professor belies a steely discipline which has put Steve's name in the headlines. Yet for all the glamour it is his family life which keeps him focused on his sailing career: Kim, a psychiatric nurse by profession, works as his campaign manager and all the children are excited by Steve's new high profile, earned since the Vendée. He has always been a dab-hand at DIY. Aged 7, he salvaged lawnmowers from rubbish dumps, before rebuilding and selling them. Aged 20 Steve dropped out of Bristol University where he was studying engineering. 'I got channelled by my parents who wanted me to get married have 2.4 kids a Ford Cortina and a nice job. It was all too much'. Instead Steve used his initiative to work as a freelance mechanic repairing motorbikes which led to a job restoring vintage cars such as Baby Rolls Royces, Lamborghinis, Aston Martins and Lagondas.

Steve started sailing aged 24 in 1996 when a friend, Richard Heaton, bought *Teal*, a 17 ft Lysander and nagged Steve to trail it to Portland for him as he had a tow bar on his car. 'All we had as a guide was the Ladybird Book of Sailing,' said Steve. Both he and Kim were soon hooked on sailing. They bought their own 17 ft Robert Tucker Ballerina, *Angharad*, and based her in Portland. After a year exploring the Dorset coast they upgraded to a Trapper 28, *Red Sox* and sailed her from Portland, with the family, to Cherbourg and back in 2000.

In 1998 when his boss at the vintage car business came back with brochures from a day out on the Solent aboard *Toshiba*, a 67 ft Whitbread Challenge Round the World Race Yacht, Steve's imagination was fired up. He paid for a berth aboard *Ocean Rover*, a Challenge 67, for a rough trip out round the Fastnet Rock and back. 'When I stood on the dockside at Plymouth after that trip, everything had come into focus for me. I decided I was going to become a professional sailor,' Steve said. He handed in his notice and got a job installing marine engines at the Ferry Bridge Boatyard in Portland. He worked for a while for Pete Goss at the Totnes Boatyard on the ill-fated *Team Philips* catamaran. Then he worked as corporate crew for Chay Blyth's Challenge business, gradually working up to skipper on £22 000 a year. During this period he sailed to the Fastnet and back 24 times. He was reserve skipper for the 2004–05 Global Challenge, but became disillusioned by the selection process to become a skipper proper. 'I refused to build a bridge out of boiled eggs or to engage in the psycho-babble of the training exercises. It was man-management stuff and nothing to do with sailing. I can't do something that's false. But if you did not play the game you did not get a boat. I did not play the game,' Steve said.

In 2007 he bought Josh Hall's old Open 60, *Gartmore*, a Finot design from 1998, with a fixed keel. Steve re-named her *Spirit of Weymouth* and in the Fastnet Race 2007 came 8th in class and 17th overall out of nearly 300 boats. The majority retired after less than 24 hours due to bad weather. In 2008 he entered her in the Artemis Transatlantic single-handed race from Plymouth to Boston and finished 9th just 85 miles behind *Aviva*, Dee Caffari's brand new state-of-the-art Open 60. Steve's budget was less than 0.2 per cent of Caffari's. But all this was just a warm up. Steve's heart was set on sailing in the Vendée Globe

2008–09. He now faced a four-year battle to get funding, a battle which saw him re-mortgage his home four times.

Steve set off from Portland and was only 15 miles out of Les Sables d'Olonne when he received a phone call from his sponsor saying: "'I'm sorry the deal's fallen through". I couldn't call Kim with the bad news because then the Iridium satphone had gone down. I felt physically sick'.

He sailed into Les Sables d'Olonne thinking he had lost his house and his boat because he had run out of time to enter the race. Once ashore he discovered another sponsor had stepped in at the last minute. He was a mystery figure who did not want any personal publicity, but wished to publicise the *Toe in the Water* campaign: a charity which helps injured servicemen and women by getting them out sailing. Steve's race was on after all. 'I was on the biggest high imaginable!' he said.

But now he faced a monumental refit before even setting off. The boat had to be hauled out for sand-blasting and re-painting. Steve also fitted new standing rigging, new sails, a generator, and a new water-maker.

'French people we had never met turned up and worked for nothing to help us get her ready,' said Steve.

A scathing report in the *Daily Telegraph* said *Toe in the Water* resembled *Teignmouth Electron*, the ill-fated, and unprepared trimaran from which Donald Crowhurst lost his life while competing in the first solo, non-stop, round-the-world race, organised by the *Sunday Times* in 1968–69.

Steve was dubbed 'the underdog' of the Vendée, but the world hadn't heard about his 'speed gene', as his wife Kim describes it. For Steve has a 'Boy's Own' enthusiasm for going fast. There must be something in the water bubbling down from the Derbyshire Peaks for Steve almost shares the birthplace of another record-breaking sailor: Dame Ellen MacArthur. She was born in Whatstandwell a village just five miles from Steve's birthplace in Wirksworth.

But despite the last-minute sponsorship, Steve's preparation for the Vendée Globe was chaotic. Even *Yachting Monthly*'s technical editor, Chris Beeson, re-christened Steve White's boat 'Steptoe in the Water' such was her scrapyard appearance. But 109 days later Steve, to massive acclaim by crowds, finished 8th in a fleet which wiped out the giants of sailing, including fellow Brit Mike Golding. Only 11 of 30 starters completed the 27 000-mile course. Steve's Corinthian approach won him a reception in Les Sables d'Olonne second only to Michel Desjoyeaux.

Fifty-thousand people chanted: 'Steve White, Steve White' as he sailed in. Walking round the streets after the race Steve was stopped continuously for his autograph, others asked him to visit their homes and schoolchildren were lifted up to kiss him. One old man came up to him, pressed 10 Euros into his hand and said: 'You sailed such a clean and beautiful race I want you to have a drink on me,' and then hugged him! Several locals asked him if he would consider moving to the town to live.

During the race Steve White entertained readers and alarmed his family in equal measure with his candid blogs on problem-solving. Here are some excerpts:

18 November 2008

I rolled around in the dirt under the chart table plugging things in and unplugging them for 40 minutes, after my old autopilot failed. It's a terrible feeling when you know that the people behind you are catching you up, and those in front are getting away as you roll around in the bilge with the soldering iron between your toes with the boat rolling like a pig towards Brazil at half a knot. Aaaargh!

28 November 2008

Last night after the mother of all squalls came through, I had a mastic spree. One of my computer screens bounced out, and the window above my bed started pouring in water, so I sealed them up, and I glued up the microphone rest for the VHF. I don't know why Sikkaflex doesn't sponsor a boat, after all, the entire marine industry would fall apart without the stuff, and I must admit, so would most of our house and our cars!

9 January 2009

At least the calm conditions have given me the chance to complete the repairs; the gooseneck is now well and truly held in place with a fairly serious piece of composite engineering and some fairly serious Dyneema lashing wound bar tight with a couple of Spanish windlasses below decks to two strong points on the keel. All the nasty cracking noises have stopped now, and I have a great deal of confidence in the repair. The generator is lashed down to some carbon dowels fitted to the bearers, as one of the mounts had ripped its bolts out and another had just sheered. That isn't going anywhere now either! I had a keel moment too – down the side of the empty fuel tank on the starboard side, I caught sight of a dirty great bolt, and had a horrible thought that it must have been one of the draw bolts that go through the keel foil and its socket inside the boat. In the end I couldn't stand it anymore, and I removed the tank and had a look – everything was fine, I think someone had just dropped a load of bolts down the side during the refit.

* * *

Reproduced with permission by *Yachting Monthly*.

THE DEAD LAY IN HER WAKE

An indecisive skipper and too little wind made for a fatal combination – but one brave woman helped ensure some crew survived

In March 1897 New Yorkers queued up to board the harbour's ferry boats and stare with amazement at a 'ghost ship' which had come back from the dead. The hulk of the iron-hulled three-master *T. F. Oakes* lay anchored in the calm waters of the harbour. Her topsides were red with rust, there was even a patina of corrosion floating around her neglected hull. The paint had long since been stripped away by wind, sun and sea.

Along the waterline, long strands of thick seaweed waved in the wash of passing steamers and leprous barnacles as big as a baby's fist covered the underwater hull like some ghastly pox. Aloft, among the torn and frayed canvas hung in poorly stowed bunches beneath her yardarms, fluttered the warning yellow Q flag for quarantine as she awaited fumigation.

For three months the *T. F. Oakes* had been listed as 'overdue' with Lloyds, and underwriters were already weighing up the cost of her foundering.

The ship had left Hong Kong with 180 days' worth of provisions and arrived in New York 259 days later. She was towed into harbour and instead of a claim for total loss, a massive salvage bill now faced her insurers.

Twelve of her crew were taken aboard the quarantine tender on stretchers, their feet swollen, their bodies discoloured, their tongues expanded and pushing out of their mouths and their teeth loose and falling out. All were victims of scurvy. Those who could walk off were being medically examined.

The wife of Captain E. W. Reed, master of the *T. F. Oakes*, and the second mate, Mr Abrams, had navigated and sailed the ship between them, for the last three weeks of the hell voyage. Her master lay helpless in his bunk, suffering from a stroke which affected his speech and which had forced him to make slurred orders to the crew via his wife. The second mate, also suffering from scurvy, was still standing, but only just. Seven of the crew, including the first mate, Stephen Bunker, had died on the passage. The others, including the third mate, were all seriously ill.

The *T. F. Oakes*, built in Philadelphia, in 1883, sailed from Hong Kong, for New York, on 5 July1896 after having loaded a cargo of hides, skins and other raw materials at Shanghai a month earlier. Her crew consisted of 26 hands, including the Captain, his wife and the three mates.

Captain Reed had prepared to take her home the normal route through the South China Sea, the Sunda Strait, and then across the Indian Ocean, to the Cape of Good Hope.

For the first six days of the passage they had fine weather, with light variable winds, and the *T. F. Oakes* made steady, but slow progress. On the seventh day the weather changed, the sky became overcast and murky, the barometer started to fall, and it soon became oppressively hot and sultry. All the omens for an impending typhoon. Sail was shortened and the ship hove-to on the starboard tack.

The typhoon twisted over the ship with exceptional fury. One minute they were becalmed, the next they were hit by a gale which increased to hurricane force within an hour.

The *T. F. Oakes*, renowned for being a sluggish performer on the deep sea routes, hove-to badly, she kept falling away from the mounting seas and rolled sideways instead into their troughs. This meant she was swept by mountainous seas fore and aft. Her main deck was continuously awash, and, the men – a poor gaggle of sailors gathered from boarding houses – refused to come out of the the fo'c'sle, until they were forced out by the belaying pin-wielding mates.

That night the wind blew everything away but the main lower topsail. By daylight it was discovered the fore and mizzen topmasts had been sprung, and that some hatch covers had been torn off. Fearing that the ship would be dismasted and the hatches stove in, Captain Reed decided to turn round and run before the wind, which was blowing from the south-west.

For 48 hours the *T. F. Oakes* ran tearing off the knots in the wrong direction and by the time the wind died, and the sky cleared, she was within 150 miles of South Cape, Formosa.

A second blast of hurricane-force wind followed, driving the ship still farther to the east and pushing her close to the Bashi Islands, which stretch north and south between Luzon and Formosa. So, fearing the proximity of land, Captain Reed again put the vessel dead before the wind – now blowing from the north-west – and ran through the Balintang Channel, out into the Pacific.

By the time the second blow was over the *T. F. Oakes* was so far out in the Pacific Ocean that her master decided to abandon the route home, and to proceed, instead, by way of Cape Horn, even though this meant a long haul across the Pacific of nearly ten thousand miles.

Then the fickle and unreliable NE trade winds set in and day after day the *T. F. Oakes* lay becalmed with her sails flat against the masts, while the sailors toiled at the braces, trying to make the best of every breath.

By the end of September the *Oakes* was little more than 600 miles to the eastward of the Gilbert Islands, on the Equator, so it had become necessary to reduce rations.

October came and went, and still the wearisome calms persisted. All day the boiling sun beat down on the unshaded decks, making the pitch in their seams bubble up like black lava. The planks of the lifeboats began to crack, and were doused with endless buckets of salt water. The iron-walled fo'c'sle, was like an oven in which the men could neither eat nor sleep. The saloon wasn't much better. The galley and tiny pantry, where the cook and steward slaved, were like blast furnaces.

Tins of bully-beef were served up as the salt pork and beef had run out, but the sailors claimed it was contaminated and refused to eat it. They collected rain-water, since the fresh water out of the tanks was running dry. But the rain-water was stagnant, the result of being stored in contaminated casks.

On 11 November the Chinese cook died, after suffering violent stomach pains. At this time the *T. F. Oakes* was in close to the Low Archipelago. Two or three inhabited islands were within reach, and the mate suggested they should obtain water and provisions from the nearest. Captain Reed declined as he was afraid that the ship would be held in quarantine, or that the crew would jump ship.

Mrs Reed was now carrying out the dead cook's duties and by the time the *T. F. Oakes* reached the 40th parallel of South latitude, half the crew, including the mate, were laid up with scurvy; and, as the rest of the men were showing symptoms of this disease, including bleeding gums, Captain Reed decided to keep the vessel under small canvas, so that his weakened crew would be able to handle it in a blow, until she was in the fine weather of the South Atlantic.

On 21 December she rounded Cape Horn, 169 days out from Hong Kong. Two-thirds of the crew were now laid up, leaving only six on deck, including the second and third mates. A hard south-westerly gale was blowing, with fierce squalls of hail and snow, making even greater demands on the ailing crew.

Mrs Reed volunteered to help out by taking a regular trick at the wheel. The first time she steered for six hours without a break, and the second mate declared that she was a better helmsman than the majority of the men aboard.

On 26 December a crewman Thomas King died of scurvy, and on 12 January, in the latitude of the River Plate, a second sailor named Thomas Olsen died of the same disease. All the way up the South American coast from the Horn the ship had experienced hard gales from the west and north-west, which pushed her eastward and away from the possibility of docking at Montevideo.

On 17 January scurvy claimed its third victim, a sailor called Thomas Judge and, on 4 February, Stephen Bunker, the first mate, also died after being in a partial coma for several days. On 9 February sailor George King died and two days later yet another sailor perished, bringing the death toll to seven. As the survivors took inventories of the dead men's clothes and effects a deep gloom descended over the ship.

When the *T. F. Oakes* was within two days' sailing of Pernambuco, Brazil, a number of the sick implored the Captain to put in there, holding out their emaciated arms for him to see their wretched condition. But he explained that now that they had come so far it was better to carry on to their destination, claiming the port was well known for exploiting American ships.

Off Trinidad an American ship named *Governor Robie* hove in sight. In response to the stricken vessel's signal, 'Short of provisions-starving,' she launched a boat and sent over food, water, tobacco and medicines. This much-needed relief came too late to bring sick men back to health, but at least they were no longer starving.

Captain Reed was the next to fall ill – not from scurvy – but from a stroke brought on by the stress of his command. He took to his bunk and the ship was now captained by the second mate and the indefatigable Mrs Reed, who was also cooking, hauling on the ropes and tending the sick men in the fo'c'sle. At the wheel she wore a large Ulster coat to keep out the cold.

The north-east trades, which had carried the *T. F. Oakes* up to the Bahamas, gave way to westerly gales, which drove her so far out into the North Atlantic that the two navigators seriously contemplated putting the ship before the wind and running for Gibraltar.

But at last on the night of 15 March, the British oil-tanker *Kasbek*, bound for the Mediterranean from Philadelphia, was steaming across the Atlantic, when suddenly the blue-light of a distress flare lit up the sea.

Captain Muirhead, the *Kasbek's* master, raised his megaphone and asked the name of the distressed ship.

'*T. F. Oakes*,' came the hoarse reply, 'Bound to New York from Hong Kong. Over eight months out. For God's sake give us a tow'.

The *Kasbek* was steaming to the east, and New York was 600 miles astern. This would be an expensive tow. So Captain Muirhead launched a boat and sent over his mate to find out what was the matter.

As this officer climbed aboard the *T. F. Oakes* he was greeted by the second mate of the sailing ship, whose hands, wrists and legs were so swollen that he was nearly helpless. There was no-one else on deck except Mrs Reed, who was at the wheel in her Ulster coat.

Having satisfied himself that the *T. F. Oakes* had a good eight-inch towing hawser, the mate returned to his own ship and a working party was sent over, to remain with the weakened crew of the *T. F. Oakes* until she had been towed into port.

Unfortunately, the slack of the three-inch hauling line got foul of the *Kasbek's* propeller and the *T. F. Oakes* had to be cast adrift as the screw was cleared, a job which lasted ten hours.

After clearing the fouled tow-rope a gale blew up and the two ships drifted further apart and it was three days after sighting the beleaguered ship that the tow finally commenced.

On Sunday morning, 21 March, just as the church bells were calling the faithful to prayer, the two vessels anchored off Fort Wadsworth, New York.

Lloyd's showed their appreciation of Mrs Reed's fortitude by presenting her with their Silver Medal for Meritorious Service.

A Court of Inquiry was set up to investigate the Captain's conduct, but he was acquitted of any blame for all the misfortunes which had befallen his ship.

Despite his exoneration by the court, Captain Reed was severely criticised in many quarters for not putting into Pernambuco or another Brazilian port.

Four years later the *T. F. Oakes*, a jinxed ship if ever there was one, was wrecked on the Californian coast.

THE TERROR OF A LEE-SHORE

American yachtsman William Albert Robinson sailed a 32 ft Bermudan ketch, *Svaap*, around the world from New York to New York in the late 1920s and early 1930s, but encountered his worst weather just off the mouth of Rome's River Tiber

He would have lost his boat and possibly his life and that of his crew but for the fact he'd bent a new set of sails on. The first signs he was to feel a midsummer storm in the Mediterranean was the classic red sky at night and a falling glass. The following day the glass dropped further and Robinson and his crew Etera, a Tahitian longshoreman Robinson had picked up in the South Seas, were exhausted from the excessive humidity and stillness which had replaced the regular breeze from the north. Then banks of cloud built up astern and a very confused sea started running as if created by some unseen diabolical machine, there was not a breath of wind. That evening the wind came. Firstly from the south-east it veered sharply into the south-west and as the sun went down again blood-red, *Svaap* was swallowed by the worst sea she'd encountered anywhere in the world.

They were now battling with a south-west gale and huge sea just 15 miles from the black rocky coastline of Italy. But the wind increased still and with a hurricane to fight the little *Svaap* was under just jib and mizzen driving slowly forward and at times driven back towards the rocks. She was heeled so far over that the heavy seas were confronted only by her sweetly round bilge which helped dash them into spray. At one time the jib started to tear away from its stay and Robinson left Etera lashed to the wheel while he went out on the bowsprit end and was plunged into the seas like a piece of fondu meat as he lashed on extra gaskets to save the sail. Without it the boat would have simply gone beam on to the blow and rolled down onto the reefs of the Old Boot.

Trying to get some rest off watch, Robinson watched the moon bouncing in horrible arcs through the porthole as he listened to the bilge water surfing up and down *Svaap's* wooden sides. He also watched with quiet desperation the shore lights of Fiumara Grande getting clearer in the night. The land was creeping closer to *Svaap's* one inch and an eighth of pitch-pine planking. But she held her own until a huge sea swept the little yacht and she staggered and disappeared completely under the water with just her masts poking out drunkenly from the maelstrom. As she lifted and the water poured off her, Etera was gone and the wheel spun free. Fortunately his harness held and Robinson dragged him back aboard.

Dawn eventually brought its relieving light and showed a hideous sea, but also a sense that the worst was over and by midday they were under full sail once more and heading for the French Riviera.

Robinson smiled to himself and thought 'In every harbour lay shining yachts large and small, but in spite of their handsome crews and the millions of their playboy owners, none had gone so far as jaunty little *Svaap*'. In all Robinson sailed the John Alden-designed *Svaap* 32 000 miles in a three and a half year-long voyage.

THE SMALLEST BOAT TO SAIL ROUND THE WORLD

Shane Acton's voyage is simply beyond belief: a circumnavigation in an 18 ft plywood bilge keeler

Not many circumnavigations start in landlocked Cambridge, England because the river there is too small to float the sort of boat you'd expect to take on an ocean voyage. But when Shane Acton, 25, set out from that hallowed university town all he could afford was £400 worth of plywood. *Super Shrimp*, was an 18 ft Caprice class bilge keeler designed to hop along the coast when the tide was in and sit up on the mud when the tide was out.

Shane's only experience of boat handling came from his time in the Royal Marine Commandos aboard landing craft. He couldn't sail when he left the Cam but by the time he'd crossed the Wash to Wells in North Norfolk he knew he had a lot to learn and port-hopped from there all the way to Falmouth, so as to avoid having to make a night passage.

He spent the winter of 1972 there moored in a drying creek and working as a builder's labourer by day and sleeping aboard *Shrimpy*, as he called his boat, by night. In June the following year he set sail and crossed the Bay of Biscay to Viana do Castelo in Portugal and port-hopped down the Portuguese coast. He then crossed the Gibraltar Strait and continued coasting down Morocco before dashing across to Las Palmas in the Canaries. Here he earned a living crewing and navigating for other sailors while he prepared *Shrimpy* for her Atlantic crossing. He made himself a self-steering system from driftwood and dumped car springs and finally set off on 23 November 1973 taking 40 days to cross the Atlantic to Barbados. Three-quarters of the way across he was woken up by the throbbing of a ship's propellers. Sticking his head out of the hatch he was amazed to find a huge freighter ranged alongside whose captain thought he'd found a lifeboat.

After an extensive cruise of the West Indies and while in the San Blas islands en route to the Panama Canal he met Iris Derungs, a young Swiss girl who became part of *Shrimpy's* crew.

Once in the Pacific they cruised down the coast of Ecuador and sailed from Guyaquil on 10 December 1974 visiting the Galapagos Islands where the breath of an investigating blue whale invaded their cabin. Three weeks later they set off for the biggest voyage of the little Thames Estuary boat's life: 3 200 miles of the Pacific Ocean. Shane used a plastic sextant to navigate and had, for the most part a trouble-free passage, even recording halfway across that while listening to the radio he heard that Wimbledon drew with Leeds in an away match!

After 45 days the boat designed for trips inside Southend Pier anchored in Taiohae Bay on the island of Nuku Hiva, main island of the Marquesas group.

Shane did not rest on the laurels of his achievement for long: this practical, self-starter soon had a job unloading the local copra schooner to raise funds for the next part of the voyage. Even so when *Shrimpy* arrived in Tahiti and her crew moored up in the main port Papeete they discovered it cost £4 just to enter the harbour. They had £1. Shane solved the problem by getting another job this time on a yacht helping prepare her for a long voyage. Iris, with her command of several languages, also landed a job working in the local duty free shop, serving the legions of tourists.

They spent two months in French Polynesia before sailing for the Cook Islands where they intended to sit out the hurricane season. After wrangling with the authorities there, Shane had *Shrimpy* lifted out onto a 'piece of grass' while the pair continued living aboard: 'We never found out who owned the land, but once a month two workmen came to cut the grass which had become our front lawn,' he said.

The resourceful skipper of the smallest boat ever to visit the Cook Islands landed a job as captain of a 60 ft fishing boat which delivered groceries to the outer islands of the group.

In Rarotonga Shane was given an old battered Seagull outboard in return for navigation lessons and for the first time since leaving Falmouth *Shrimpy* had an engine.

By July 1976 the pair had reached Fiji and in October that year they reached Brisbane where *Shrimpy* was lifted out of the sea and plonked in a friend's swimming pool in preparation for a visit by the Duke of Edinburgh who was impressed with the cockleshell so far from home.

They sailed from Brisbane 1500 miles up the coast of eastern Australia inside the Great Barrier Reef and from September 1977 until June the following year they wintered in Gove, in the Northern Territories of Australia, to ride out the next hurricane season. Here Shane landed a job dismantling pre-fabricated houses which helped to pay for replacing *Shrimpy's* keel bolts which had rusted through.

Bali in Indonesia held no charm for Shane as Iris left *Shrimpy* to return home to Switzerland to visit her mother and would not be rejoining the ship until she reached the Mediterranean. So Shane was solo again crossing the Indian Ocean via Sri Lanka to Mangalore and then across the Arabian Sea from Mangalore to Djibouti.

Using his outboard Shane hopped up the Red Sea along the Saudi Arabian coastline until finally the boat which should never have crossed the world was almost shipwrecked when she jumped off a large wave and split a plywood panel in her bottom. Shane managed to beach her on the Sinai Peninsula and repair the panel.

He transited the Suez Canal and sailed to Larnaca, Cyprus where an English yachtsman asked him if he had sailed all the way there from England to the Mediterranean. 'Yes, the long way round,' answered Shane.

'Oh you mean via Gibraltar and not the French canals?'

'No, I mean via the Atlantic, Panama, the Pacific, Australia, the Indian Ocean, Red Sea and the Suez Canal,' said Shane.

Few believed him, others thought he was joking.

Iris rejoined the boat on the Greek island of Symi and together they took the boat through the Med up the French canals and back to the UK via the Channel Islands, clearing customs in Ramsgate.

Finally in August 1980 *Super Shrimp* arrived back in Cambridge after an eight-year circumnavigation.

BIBLIOGRAPHY

Chapter 1

Desperate Voyage, John Caldwell, Victor Gollancz, 1952.

Chapter 2

117 Days Adrift, by Maurice and Maralyn Bailey, Nautical Publishing, 1974.

Chapter 3

Famous Sea Tragedies, Valentine Dyall, Arrow Books, 1957.

Chapter 4

Epics of the Square Rigged Ships, edited by Charles Domville-Fife, published by Seeley Service, 1958.

Chapter 5

Once is Enough, Miles Smeeton, Rupert Hart-Davis, 1959.

Chapter 6

South: the Story of Shackleton's Last Expedition 1914–1917, Pimlico, 1999.

Chapter 7

Shipping Wonders of the World Volume II, edited by Clarence Winchester, published by Fleetway House, 1936.

Chapter 8

Last Voyage, Readers Union William Heinemann, 1953.

Chapter 9

Shipping Wonders of the World Volume II, edited by Clarence Winchester, published by Fleetway House, 1936.

Chapter 10

Adrift, Steven Callahan, Guild Publishing, 1986.

Chapter 11

Epics of the Square Rigged Ships, edited by Charles Domville-Fife, published by Seeley Service, 1958.

Chapter 12

MingMing and the Art of Minimal Ocean Sailing by Roger D Taylor, The Fitzroy Press, 2010.

Chapter 13

Down Channel, R. T. McMullen, Rupert Hart-Davis, 1949.

Chapter 14

The Marine Accident Investigation Branch Report and an interview with Michael Dresden by Dick Durham for Yachting Monthly.

Chapter 15

The Magic of the Swatchways, by Maurice Griffiths, published by Adlard Coles Nautical, 2000.

Chapter 16

Fastnet Force 10, John Rousmaniere, Nautical, 1980.

Chapter 17

The Wandering Years, by Weston Martyr, William Blackwood, 1940.

Chapter 18

Sailing, A Course of My Life, by Edward Heath, Sidgwick & Jackson, 1975.

Chapter 19

The War with Cape Horn, Alan Villiers, Hodder & Stoughton, 1971.

Chapter 20

Ice Bird, David Lewis, Adlard Coles Nautical, 1975.

Chapter 21

Coasting Bargemaster, A. W.Roberts, Seafarer Books, 2000.

Chapter 22

Just Sea & Sky, Ben Pester, Adlard Coles Nautical, 2010.

Chapter 23

Heroes of the Goodwin Sands, fourth edition, T Stanley Treanor, The Religious Tract Society, 1893.

Chapter 24

Peyton, Dick Durham, Adlard Coles Nautical, 2009.

Chapter 25

North Sea Fishers & Fighters, Walter Wood, Kegan Paul, Trench, Trubner & Co 1911.

Chapter 26

Hands Open, by Les Powles, published by Kenneth Mason Publications, 1987.

Chapter 27

A White Boat from England, George Millar, William Heinemann, 1951.

Chapter 28

The Cruise of the Cachalot, Frank T Bullen, 10th impression, second edition, published by Smith, Elder & Co, 1902.

Chapter 29

The Cruise of the *Alerte*, E.F. Knight, Thomas Nelson.

Chapter 30

The Kon-Tiki Expedition, Thor Heyerdahl, Allen & Unwin, 1952.

Chapter 31

Drake, by Ernle Bradford, published by Hodder & Stoughton, 1965.

Chapter 32

Sailing Just for Fun, Charles Stock, Seafarer Books, 2002.

Chapter 33

The Cruise of the *Teddy*, Erling Tambs, George Newnes, 1937.

Chapter 34

Yachting Monthly, Dick Durham.

Chapter 35

Ocean-Crossing Wayfarer, Frank & Margaret Dye, David & Charles, 1977.

Chapter 36

The Incredible Voyage, Tristan Jones, Adlard Coles Nautical, 1996.

Chapter 37

Francis Chichester, Anita Leslie, Hutchinson, 1975.

Chapter 38

The Strange Voyage of Donald Crowhurst, by Nicholas Tomalin and Ron Hall, Adlard Coles. Dick Durham and Paul Gelder, Yachting Monthly.

Chapter 39

Yachting Monthly, Dick Durham.

Chapter 40

Shipping Wonders of the World Volume II, edited by Clarence Winchester, published by Fleetway House, 1936.

Chapter 41

Shipping Wonders of the World Volume II, edited by Clarence Winchester, published by Fleetway House, 1936.

Chapter 42

Famous Sea Tragedies, Valentine Dyall, Arrow Books 1957.

Chapter 43

The Riddle of the Sands, by Erskine Childers With Historical Postscript, by R. M. Bowker, Bowker & Betram, 1976.

Chapter 44

Epics of the Square Rigged Ships, edited by Charles Domville-Fife, published by Seeley Service, 1958.

Chapter 45

Close To The Wind, by Pete Goss, Headline Book Publishing, 1998.

Chapter 46

Wandering Under Sail, Eric Hiscock, Robert Ross & Co in association with George G Harrap, revised and enlarged edition 1948.

Chapter 47

The Loneliest Race, by Paul Gelder, published by Adlard Coles Nautical, 1995.

Chapter 48

Sailing Alone Across the Atlantic (a pensioner's tale), Trevor Wilson, Melrose Books, 2008. And interviews with Dick Durham for Yachting Monthly.

Chapter 49

The Cruise of the Cachalot, Frank T Bullen, 10th impression, second edition, published by Smith, Elder & Co, 1902.

Chapter 50

Come Wind or Weather, Clare Francis, published by Sphere Books, 1979.

Chapter 51

Sailing Alone Around the World, Joshua Slocum, Adlard Coles Nautical, 2006.

Chapter 52

The Log of the *Cutty Sark*, Basil Lubbock, Brown Son & Ferguson, 1966.

Chapter 53

A World of my Own, Sir Robin Knox-Johnston, Adlard Coles, 2004.

Chapter 54

The Trouble With Cruising, J.D.Sleightholme, Nautical Books, 1982.

Chapter 55

Sailing Barges, Frank G.G.Carr, 1989.

Chapter 56

The Fight of the *Firecrest*, Alain Gerbault, Hodder & Stoughton, 1929; In Quest of the Sun, Alain Gerbault, Hodder & Stoughton, 1929.

Chapter 57

Yachting Monthly, from an interview by Dick Durham.

Chapter 58

Epics of the Square Rigged Ships, edited by Charles Domville-Fife, published by Seeley Service, 1958.

Chapter 59

Deep Water And Shoal, William Albert Robinson, Jonathan Cape, re-printed May 1943.

Chapter 60

Shrimpy, Shane Acton, Patrick Stephens, Cambridge, 1981.